THE BOMBER IN WORLD WAR II

ALFRED PRICE

THE BOMBER
IN WORLD WAR II

CHARLES SCRIBNER'S SONS
NEW YORK

Contents

Foreword

by Air Chief Marshal Sir Ralph Cochrane AFC FRAeS

Air Officer Commanding No 3 (Bomber) Group, September 1942 to February 1943, No 5 (Bomber) Group February 1943 to January 1945

The author has once again shown his skill in handling technical details. Descriptions such as those contained in this book, not only of the bomber aircraft and the tactics they employed, but also of their armament and the electronic measures and counter-measures which accompanied the offensive, cannot fail to be of interest to historians of the future. For the bomber offensive of the Second World War is almost certainly unique, since it was appropriate to a stage of aeronautical development which has now passed.

It is clear that much original research has gone into the making of this account, which is a mine of useful information.

SHIPTON-UNDER-WYCHWOOD
MARCH 1976

Introduction

My aim in putting together this book has been to show, in general terms, how the bomber aircraft and its tactics evolved during the Second World War. This is a vast subject, and to cover it within the confines of a book this size I have had to stick very closely to the 'kernel' of the bomber genre. For this reason I have avoided descriptions of aircraft and tactics employed in such fringe roles as torpedo and specialized anti-shipping operations, anti-submarine operations, and ground attack operations; and, because the single-engined bomber types were associated mainly with such operations, I have confined the descriptions in this account to multi-engined aircraft. As in my previous book *World War II Fighter Conflict*, to which this is a sequel, I have made no attempt to describe every bomber type which went into service nor every tactical innnovation. Instead, I have concentrated on giving the reader a picture of the general pattern of technical and tactical developments during the six years of war. As I trust the reader will agree after reading a few pages, even allowing for these constraints there is still ample scope for a fascinating story of human endeavour.

In preparing this book I have been fortunate in being able to draw on the massive experience of some of the leading experts in their respective fields: on questions of aerodynamics Sir Morien Morgan, CB, MA, FRS, ex-director of the Royal Aircraft Establishment at Farnborough; on structures Dr Percy Walker, CBE, PhD, FRAeS, ex-head of the structures department at Farnborough; on power plants Mr D. McCarthy, BSc, the Chief Engineering Staff Engineering, Rolls Royce Ltd; and on bomber tactics Air Chief Marshal Sir Ralph Cochrane, GBE, KCB, FRAeS, who commanded No 3 then No 5 Groups of RAF Bomber Command during the war. I am deeply grateful for the help I have received from these gentlemen, but I must stress that I alone am responsible for the opinions expressed in this book.

The Crown Copyright documents held in the Public Record Office in London are quoted by permission of the Controller of Her Majesty's Stationary Office.

In collecting the material and photographs for this book I have received help from many good friends. In particular, I should like to express my thanks to Harl Brackin of Boeing, Horst Goetz, Walter Brieke, Hanfried Schliephake, Wolfgang Dierich, John Taylor, Franz Selinger, Kenneth Munson and Jim Oughton. Last, but certainly not least, I should like to thank Peter Endsleigh Castle for the hard work and imagination he has put into the line drawings.

ALFRED PRICE
Uppingham, Rutland
March 1976

In this book the aircraft weights stated are those for normal operation, not the overload condition. The miles given are statute miles and speeds are given in statute miles per hour. The maximum speeds are quoted for each bomber type only for comparative purposes; during operations bombers usually flew at their economical cruising speed, which was approximately two thirds of the maximum speed. The effective operational radii given are approximate figures, intended only as a basis for comparison; they are based on the best available figures in each case, adjusted for a 2,000 pound bomb load where appropriate, and allow sufficient reserve fuel for one hour's flight at economical cruising speed. The weapon calibres given are those usually used for the weapon being described, ie the .303-in Browning or the 20 mm Oerlikon cannon.

1. The Means of Destruction

*The means of destruction are approaching
perfection with frightening rapidity.*

JOMINI: Précis de l'Art de la Guerre, 1838

During the decade which began in 1929 there was a revolution in the design of bomber aircraft. Within those ten years speeds, ranges, operating altitudes and the loads carried were all more than doubled. In no similar period, either before or since, have so many far-reaching changes been incorporated into aircraft in such a rapid succession. It was as though designers all over the world had suddenly been able to tear themselves free of the bonds which had fettered them almost since the beginning of flight.

Before considering the nature and the effects of the various changes introduced during the 1930s, however, it might be as well to take a brief look at the capabilities of bombers before 'the great leap forward'.

Representative of the latest type of bomber in 1929 was the Handley Page Hinaidi which had just entered service in the Royal Air Force. Constructed of a metal framework covered with fabric, the Hinaidi was a biplane with a wing span of just over 75 feet. Two Bristol Jupiter engines provided power for the Hinaidi; each developed 440 horse power at normal revolutions, though at a pinch they could be squeezed to give 550 horse power. This rotational power was converted into thrust by two wooden four-bladed airscrews, whose pitch angle at two-thirds radius was immovably set at just over 21 degrees; this angle was a compromise between the conflicting requirements of fine pitch for take-off and coarse pitch for maximum speed. As a result, there was a measure of inefficiency at either end of the speed scale. The engines lacked superchargers which meant that, as the aircraft climbed higher, the pressure of the fuel-air mixture entering the cylinders was reduced and power gradually fell. Normally laden the bomber had a maximum speed of 115 mph at 5,000 feet, falling to 98 mph at 15,000 feet.

Cruising at a stately 75 mph at 5,000 feet and carrying its maximum bomb load of 1,500 pounds, the Hinaidi had an effective attack radius of about 100 miles; if two-thirds of the bombs were left off and an equivalent weight of fuel was carried instead, the effective attack

Representative of the latest bombers in service in 1929 was the Handley Page Hinaidi of the Royal Air Force. Powered by two 550 horse power Bristol Jupiter engines, it had a maximum speed of 115 mph; carrying 1,500 pounds of bombs, it had an effective operating radius of about 100 miles.

radius went up to about 275 miles with 500 pounds of bombs.

The Hinaidi's four-man crew sat in open positions, which enabled them to sense to the full the draughty exhilaration of flying. For its defence the bomber carried three hand-operated machine guns in nose, dorsal and ventral positions. The bombsight was the Course Setting Mark VII, a vector type sight* which under peacetime conditions gave highly accurate results: flying at 10,000 feet at speeds around 85 mph, trained crews were able to place half of their bombs within 50 yards of the target during daylight exercises. This sight was not gyroscopically stabilized, which meant that to align his aircraft on the target during the bombing run the pilot had to make flat (ie unbanked) turns.

Normally loaded the Hinaidi weighed 12,700 pounds, which gave a wing loading at take-off of about 8.5 pounds per square foot. Since the aircraft had a landing speed of only 55 mph, flaps and wheelbrakes were not considered necessary and were not fitted. The four-wheel main undercarriage was fixed, each wheel with its own shock-absorber leg; at the rear there was a tail-skid which provided a mild braking action during landings on grass airfields.

So much for the state of the art of bombers in service in 1929. Now let us examine the changes that did so much to improve performance and load-carrying ability during the crucible years that followed.

First and foremost, there was a marked improvement in aero engines. During the decade between 1925 and 1935, engine powers increased by about half as much again. More to the point, so far as bombers were concerned, these extra powers were not bought at great expense in terms of extra weight or disproportionately high fuel consumption; engine weight per horse power went down by more than a fifth and fuel consumption per horse power dropped by a similar figure.

The more efficient engines provided an

impetus for change, but alone they would not have been sufficient to bring about any major improvement in performance. Had it to haul the Hinaidi's enormous frame through the air, the extra power would have dissipated itself in overcoming the extra drag induced by flying just a little faster; and the range and load-carrying performance would have suffered accordingly, because a lot more fuel would have had to be burned to move the aircraft that little faster.

With the extra power, therefore, there had to be a ruthless cleaning-up of the bomber's aerodynamic shape. The greatest single avoidable cause of drag was the fixed undercarriage; on aircraft like the Hinaidi this constituted about 15 per cent of the bomber's total profile drag. For a little extra weight, the main wheels could be retracted neatly out of the way in the engine nacelles.

Next to go was the biplane wing arrangement; the struts and wires to keep on the top wing gave about half as much drag as the undercarriage. To maintain wing loading at the same low figure as that of a biplane, a monoplane of similar weight would have needed a wing with an area as great as that of the biplane's two wings. But by the early 1930s people could see the advantages of using a somewhat smaller unbraced cantilever wing: it would cause a lot less drag during the cruising phase of the flight, which in turn meant a reduced fuel consumption for a given speed and therefore the range or the bomb load could be increased. The attendant rise in landing speeds, resulting from the use of higher wing loadings, was accepted in the name of progress. The pilots would simply have to sharpen up a bit.

Wing loadings began to rise greatly, but the pains and penalties resulting from this were cushioned by three further innovations: braked wheels, wing flaps and variable-pitch propellers.

The advantages of braked wheels for aircraft, when landing speeds began to increase, are obvious enough. Flaps, by increasing the lift coefficient and therefore the lift of a wing by 50 per cent or more when they were lowered, made it possible for designers to use still smaller

*The different types of bombsight are discussed in the section Sighting the Bombs, page 76.

wings and yet higher wing loadings and still achieve a given landing speed. Partially lowered, flaps enabled bombers to take off with loads they could not otherwise have carried; fully lowered, they allowed flight at lower speeds and also served as air brakes to reduce 'float' during landing. Once they had become accepted, flaps began to get quite clever. When they were extended, the Fowler and Gouge types of flap moved into a position behind as well as below the trailing edge of the wing; thus the lowered flap effectively increased a wing's area by as much as a quarter and almost doubled its lift coefficient. Everything helped.

The introduction of the variable-pitch propeller removed the gross inefficiencies in converting engine power into thrust, at the high speed and low speed ends of the aircraft's performance envelope. For bombers this was particularly important: it meant that less engine power was wasted at take-off or during the cruising phase of the flight, with the result that each gallon of fuel carried the aircraft that much further. To put figures to the improvement in performance which resulted,

The Martin B-10, which entered service with the US Army Air Corps in 1934, represented a milestone in bomber development. Powered by two 775 horse power Wright Cyclone engines, it had a maximum speed of 213 mph; carrying 2,000 pounds of bombs, it had an effective operating radius of about 300 miles. *Martin*

18

let us observe what happened to a typical twin-engined aircraft of the 1930s when variable pitch propellers were fitted in place of those with a fixed pitch: take-off run was reduced by 20 per cent, rate of climb was increased by 22 per cent and cruising speed and range (for no extra fuel consumed) increased by more than 5 per cent. Such an offer in improved performance, for very little extra weight, was one no bomber designer could afford to refuse. Moreover, once the idea of a variable pitch propeller was accepted, it was a simple next stage to make the blades 'feather': by turning the blades until they were edge on to the airflow, their drag could be reduced to a minimum if the engine failed.

A further move which did much to increase the range and load-carrying ability of bombers was the universal introduction of the supercharger for engines. This enabled a greater mass of fuel-air mixture to be squeezed into the cylinders at high altitude, where the rarefied air would otherwise have caused a progressive fall in engine power. As a result engines were able to deliver their full power at altitudes far greater than would otherwise have been the case. So far as bombers were concerned, this conferred several advantages. Rarefied air is great stuff through which to make long range flights, because for a given aircraft shape it causes less drag; so the aircraft can fly faster on the same power and further on the same amount of fuel. And if flying higher made things that much more difficult for the enemy gun and fighter defences, so much the better.

During the early 1930s, also, the fabric-covered airframe began to go out of favour. It was clear that the all-metal stressed skin method of construction gave many advantages over the simple skeleton covered in fabric; it

The PZL 37B was the most modern bomber in service with the Polish Air Force at the beginning of the war and it compared well with those in service in other air forces. Powered by two 918 horse power Bristol Pegasus engines built under licence, it had a maximum speed of 276 mph; carrying 2,000 pounds of bombs, it had an effective operational radius of about 750 miles. *IWM*

was both stiffer and stronger, for a given weight. Moreover, since it was impossible to avoid some lateral ridges on the outside of a fabric-covered aircraft, the drag of the latter was always somewhat higher than that of a similarly sized machine of all-metal construction.

In 1932 Glen Martin put nearly all of the innovations into his Model 123 bomber. When the developed aircraft entered service in the US Army Air Corps as the B-10, in 1934, it was by far the most modern bomber in use by any air force. An unbraced cantilever monoplane of all-metal construction, it was fitted with a retractable undercarriage with braked main wheels, and had flaps and variable-pitch airscrews; the only thing missing was supercharging for the engines, though even this was experimented with.

That the B-10 now looks so ordinary serves only to confirm the farsightedness of Martin and his design team; for this aircraft was to set the pattern for multi-engined bomber design for the decade to follow. To reduce drag to a minimum the crew positions were enclosed, the bombs were housed in an internal bay and the nose gunner was provided with an enclosed turret from which to fire his gun. Powered by two 775 horse power radials, the B-10B had a maximum speed of 213 mph at 6,000 feet. Cruising at about 130 mph it could carry a bomb load of just over 2,200 pounds to an effective operating radius of about 300 miles. The defensive armament comprised three .3-in machine guns. Normally loaded the B-10 weighed 16,400 pounds; its wing loading was 24 pounds per square foot at take-off — three times greater than that of the Hinaidi.

At its maximum speed the B-10 did not allow any fighter then in service a sufficient margin to carry out an interception. This moved the Assistant Chief of the US Army Air Corps, Brigadier General Oscar Westover, to comment that 'No known agency can frustrate the accomplishment of a bombardment mission'. The British Prime Minister Stanley Baldwin put it another way when he stated 'The bomber will always get through'. Even before the B-10 had entered service, the ideas incorporated in it were being copied and improved upon in design offices all over the world. The shapes were being finalised for the bomber aircraft which were to equip air forces for the greater part of the Second World War.

As well as setting a cracking pace for others designing bombers, the B-10 put a metaphorical bomb under those responsible for the procurement and design of fighters. The results of this explosion are described in the companion volume *World War II Fighter Conflict*. Suffice it here to state the old Russian proverb: 'As the forest grew, the axe-handles grew also'.

The 'State of the Art' in 1939

To observe the effect of the technological advances between 1934 and 1939, we shall now examine the six most modern bombers in service when the Second World War began in September 1939: the German Junkers 88, the British Wellington and the French Loiré et Olivier 45, the Japanese Mitsubishi G3M2 and the Russian Tupolev SB-2, all twin-engined aircraft, and the Boeing B-17 four-engined bomber.

At the beginning of the war the best all round twin-engined bomber was the Junkers 88A-1, which had just entered service in the Luftwaffe. Though it had basically the same layout as the Martin B-10, the results of the previous years' progress were clearly evident. The Ju 88 was powered by two Jumo 211B liquid-cooled inverted V-12 engines, each of 35 litres and developing 1,200 horse power for take off. To maintain this power in the rarefied air at high altitude, each engine was fitted with a mechanically-driven two speed supercharger with a higher gear which cut in automatically as the aircraft climbed above 10,000 feet. Although at first glance the Jumo engines fitted to the Ju 88 might appear to be radials they were, in fact, liquid-cooled in-lines. The radiators for the cooling liquid were neatly mounted on the front of the engine, thus effectively removing the former from the

A Ju 88 loaded with four 550-pound bombs on the external underwing racks. On the port side of the nose can be seen the window in the floor under the pilot's position, through which he observed his target as he ran in prior to the dive bombing attack. Through the window on the front of the blister under the starboard side of the nose may be seen the sighting telescope for the Lotfe tachometric bombsight used for horizontal attacks. *Obert*

above the other in the two small internal bomb bays. This gave a nice compact bomb stowage situated about the aircraft's centre of gravity and there was little or no trim change when the bombs were released. The disadvantages of this arrangement were that bombs larger than 110 pounds had to be carried externally, with a resultant drag penalty; and if for any reason one of the lower bombs failed to release, the aircraft had to return home with those bombs mounted above it.

For its defence the Ju 88A-1 carried three hand-held rifle calibre machine guns; one fired forwards from the front of the cabin, one fired rearwards and upwards from the rear of the cabin and the third fired rearwards and downwards from the underneath gondola. The weapon used was the ·Rheinmetall-Borsig MG 15, a 7.9mm weapon with a rate of fire of about 1,000 rounds per minute. As a gun it was efficient enough, though it did suffer the disadvantage of being fed by 75-round saddle magazines each of which contained sufficient ammunition for only about four seconds' firing. Thus in a prolonged engagement the gunner was faced with the dilemma of either

The Rheinmetall-Borsig MG 15 machine gun, of calibre 7.9 mm, three of which were fitted to the Ju 88A-1 for self-defence. The 75-round saddle magazine allowed only four seconds' firing.

Inside the cramped cockpit of the Ju 88, showing the pilot's and observer's positions (nearest the camera). *KG 76 Archive*

changing magazines after each burst and having half-empty magazines all over the place, or leaving the magazine on his gun until it was empty — in which case it would take him five seconds to fit a new one perhaps in the middle of an engagement. The defensive armament fitted to the Ju 88A-1 was generally comparable with that carried by bombers in many other air forces; and in any case it was hoped that this bomber was fast enough to ensure that the guns would not be needed often.

As was the tendency in German bombers of the Second World War period, the four-man crew of the Ju 88 were housed close together in the nose. The wartime British propaganda line, sometimes repeated in postwar accounts, had it that this close proximity was in some way necessary to sustain morale. In fact, as anyone will testify who has operated on board a multi-seat combat aircraft, close proximity of the crew makes possible efficient operation with a minimum of distracting 'intercom natter'.

The Ju 88A-1 carried a normal maximum fuel load of 367 Imp (442 US) gallons in the four wing tanks, one on each side of the engines. For extended range flights extra fuel tanks could be fitted in each of the bomb bays. During the Spanish Civil War the Luftwaffe had learned the hard way that ordinary light alloy fuel tanks were extremely vulnerable to holing from enemy shell fragments or bullets. Thus deprived of some of its fuel, an aircraft might have insufficient for it to regain friendly territory. But there were other dangers, more immediate and more spectacular, if the tanks were hit. Fuel leaking from a tank was liable to catch fire, and then the chances were slim indeed of the aircraft remaining airborne for more than a couple of minutes before something important, like a wing, burned away. Less likely, though it sometimes happened, was an explosion in the tank itself if the correct fuel-air mixture was present above the fuel and this was ignited.

The provision of armour protection for the tanks conferred too high a weight penalty to gain much support. So before the war inventors in several countries dabbled with tanks which would re-seal themselves if they were holed and the fuel started to leak out. Only in Germany, however, were such self-sealing tanks being fitted to bombers as standard equipment prior to the beginning of the Second World War. The tank fitted to the Ju 88, amongst others, was made of compressed cellulose fibre with a wall thickness of 2mm. The self-sealing outer covering comprised a series of layers, from inside to out: 3mm thick chrome leather; 3mm thick unvulcanised rubber; two layers of lightly

The French Loiré et Olivier 451 was the fastest bomber in service at the beginning of the war. Powered by two 1,060 horse power Gnome-Rhône 14N radials, it had a maximum speed of 307 mph; carrying 2,000 pounds of bombs, it had an effective operational radius of about 450 miles. In the dorsal position the aircraft carried a Hispano 20 mm cannon, the most powerful weapon to be employed for bomber defence at that time.

This turreted defensive armament conferred four great advantages over the simpler hand-held weapons fitted to the Ju 88: firstly, the Wellington's paired weapons provided double the fire power; secondly the turrets allowed considerably greater fields of fire because the turret moved the gun round the gunner, rather than the gunner having to move the gun round its fixed mounting point; thirdly, since his turret was powered, the gunner could train his weapons on fighters coming in from the side without having to struggle with the slipstream; and fourthly the turrets used belted ammunition, so there was no need for the gunner to change magazines in combat. At the beginning of the war the Royal Air Force was very proud of the defensive armament fitted to its latest bombers; no other air force had developed powered gun turrets to anything like the same extent. Soon after the conflict began, however, it became clear that even the Wellington's defensive armament fell far short of what was necessary. The rifle-calibre machine gun, even in pairs or later in quadruple installations, was not powerful enough to ward off attacks by modern fighters flown by determined pilots.

The fastest bomber in service at the beginning of the war was the French Loiré et Olivier 451, an extremely clean aircraft in the same weight category as the Wellington but with an unladen maximum speed of 307 mph; with 2,000 pounds of bombs, its effective radius of action was about 450 miles. The defensive armament of the LeO 451 is of particular interest because, alone amongst the bombers then in service, it carried a 20mm cannon. The Hispano 404 cannon fitted on an electro-hydraulically powered mounting in the dorsal position fired 4.4-ounce rounds at a rate of 700 per minute with a muzzle velocity of 2,820 feet per second; it was a powerful weapon, with a fire-power eight times that of any of the rifle-calibre machine guns then in use for bomber defence, and certainly had enough punch to stop an enemy fighter in its tracks if one or two

The Japanese Navy's Mitsubishi G3M2 (later code-named 'Nell') had the best range performance of the twin-engined bombers in service at the beginning of the war, with an effective operational radius of over 900 miles carrying its maximum bomb load of 1,760 pounds of bombs. Powered by two 1,075 horse power Kinsei radials, it had a maximum speed of 216 mph. *IWM*

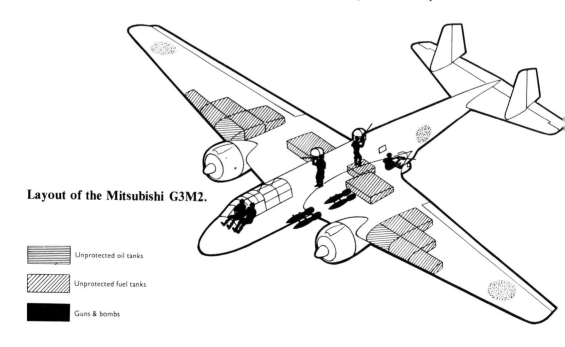

Layout of the Mitsubishi G3M2.

Unprotected oil tanks

Unprotected fuel tanks

Guns & bombs

The Russian Tupolev SB-2 was the only bomber in large-scale service at the beginning of the war to carry armour protection. The SB-2bis, depicted, was powered by two 960 horse power M-103 in-line engines and had a maximum speed of 280 mph; carrying 2,000 pounds of bombs, it had an effective operational radius of about 200 miles. *IWM*

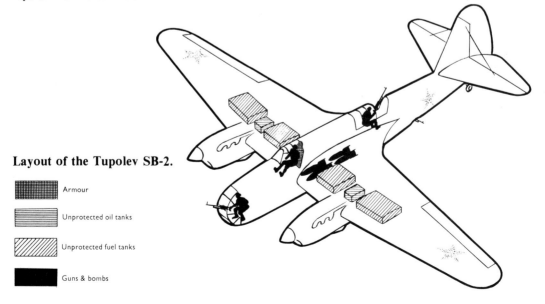

Layout of the Tupolev SB-2.

Armour

Unprotected oil tanks

Unprotected fuel tanks

Guns & bombs

The American Boeing B-17A was the only modern four-engined heavy bomber in service at the beginning of the war. Powered by four 930 horse power Wright Cyclone radials, it had a maximum speed of 256 mph; carrying 2,000 pounds of bombs, it had an effective operational radius of about 900 miles.

rounds hit it. In action, however, the gun position proved disappointing. The cannon's field of fire was limited and intercepting fighters had little difficulty in keeping out of its reach; also, the hefty 30-round magazines were difficult to change in combat. The rest of the defensive armament fitted to the LeO 451 was rather ineffectual, comprising a single 7.5mm machine gun fixed to fire forwards and another of these weapons in a retractable 'dustbin' position under the nose.

On the other side of the world the Japanese Navy was operating the remarkable Mitsubishi G3M2 Model 21 (later given the Allied code-name Nell). To squeeze the maximum range performance out of the bomber with only a pair of 1,075 horse power engines to haul it through the air, the Mitsubishi design team had to do some drastic weight pruning to get their bomber to go further than similarly-sized bombers of other nations. By cutting structural weight to the limit and reducing safety margins they held the unladen weight of the G3M2 to below 11,000 pounds — about a third less than in the case of the Ju 88, the Wellington and the LeO 451 at a time when, it should be stressed, the latter were not carrying armour either. The resultant bomber was a 'this side up handle with care' sort of aeroplane, able to lift a prodigious amount of fuel. With 1,760 pounds (880 kg) of bombs carried externally the G3M2 had an effective radius of action of just over 900 miles, a remarkable achievement for a twin-engined aircraft of this period. To reduce drag during the long cruising flights the cupolas over the three gun positions, two on the upper fuselage and one beneath it, each with a single 7.7mm machine gun, could be retracted to fit almost flush with the skin. In spite of the unkind remarks made at this time that the Japanese were copyists lacking ideas of their own, the Mitsubishi design team had demonstrated considerable originality in the G3M2. They had pursued their quest for a long-range bomber with single-mindedness and determination; the results of their labour would present their enemies with some nasty shocks when war came to the Pacific.

In 1939 the only bomber in large-scale service

fitted with armour was the Russian Tupolev SB-2; and in its case the armour was limited to an 8mm thick steel back to the pilot's seat. The fuel tanks fitted to the bomber were not self-sealing. The SB-2bis, the main production version at the time, had a maximum speed of 280 mph and had an effective operational radius of about 200 miles carrying 2,000 pounds of bombs. A variant of the SB-2, designated the SB-RK, was strengthened and fitted with dive brakes to enable it to carry out dive-bombing attacks. Compared with that of the Junkers 88, however, the attack system was very much a 'do it yourself' affair.

The only modern heavy bomber in service in September 1939 was the American B-17 Flying Fortress, a four-engined machine in a class of its own. The Boeing B-17A was impressively larger than any other bomber then in service, with normal maximum take-off weight of 42,600 pounds — nearly twice as great as that of the Ju 88A-1. Powered by four 930 horse power Wright Cyclone radials, it had a maximum speed of 256 mph at 14,000 feet. With a 2,000 pound bomb load it had an effective operating radius of about 900 miles. For its defence the early versions of the B-17 carried five hand-held .3-in machine guns, one each in the nose, mid-upper, ventral and the two waist gun positions.

The latest version of the Flying Fortress, the B-17B which was on the point of entering service when the war began in Europe, featured turbo-superchargers; the latter greatly improved its high altitude performance and effectively increased the bomber's optimum operating altitude from 14,000 feet to 25,000 feet. Initially the turbo-superchargers were unreliable; and the early versions of the B-17 were poorly armed compared with those which came later. The significance of this aircraft, however, was that it was a basically sound design that would be capable of development into something much better when the need arose.

So much for the six bomber types which can be said to represent the zenith in design, of those in service in September 1939. We shall now consider the path of evolution of the bomber aircraft during the six years that followed, from the standpoints of aerodynamics, structures, engines and armament.

The Shape of the Bomber

Throughout the Second World War there was a remarkable similarity in the shape of multi-engined bombers: the 'basic B-10 layout' reigned supreme. The only serious departure from this was in Italy, where Savoia Marchetti and CANT produced three-engined designs with the third engine mounted on the nose. Yet this was primarily a means of squeezing reasonable performance out of low-powered engines, rather than because of any intrinsic merit of the three-engined layout.

Early in the war heavy bombers evolved into two distinct types: those which relied on their defensive armament to fight their way through the enemy fighter defences by day, and those which operated under cover of darkness endeavouring to avoid the enemy defences so far as was possible. The two schools are exemplified by the American B-17 and the British Lancaster, respectively. Both aircraft were in about the same category as regards normal maximum take-off weight, tipping the scales at about 60,000 pounds; and in each case there was about 25,000 pounds available for the carriage of fuel, bombs, defensive guns and armour. The B-17 was able to carry 3,500 pounds of bombs to Berlin by day and had a defensive armament weighing 6,500 pounds, the Lancaster was able to carry 8,500 pounds of bombs to Berlin by night and had a defensive armament weighing 3,000 pounds.

During the conflict there was a continuation of the trends that had been established before it. Wings became progressively smaller for the weight they had to carry and wing loadings steadily increased. At the beginning of the war the Wellington 1A had a maximum wing loading of 33 pounds per square foot and that

Italian Savoia Marchetti 79 bombers; the designers used the three-engined layout because it was the only way they could achieve a reasonable performance on the 750 horse power available from the Alfa Romeo 126 radial. In this they were successful: the SM 79 had a maximum speed of 267 mph; carrying 2,000 pounds of bombs, it had an effective operational radius of about 600 miles. *Selinger*

STAGE I.		The new bomber has beautifully clean lines.
STAGE II.		The 5 m.p.h. loss in speed is more than compensated by the improvement in rear view so that one can see if the enemy is overtaking.
STAGE III.		The loss in speed due to the larger bomb doors is negligible (5 m.p.h.)
STAGE IV.		If the aircraft is to defend itself it must be capable of doing so in any direction—the loss in performance is negligible, the cruising speed being reduced by only 5 m.p.h.
STAGE V.		Navigational aids are of course essential—the maximum reduction of speed is certainly not more than 5 m.p.h.
STAGE VI.		Radio equipment is essential in these days—the various items are added separately and none affects the performance adversely to any greater extent than 5 m.p.h.
STAGE VII.		If one aircraft can be saved by the addition of a simple device whose effect on performance is negligible then IT IS WORTH IT.
STAGE VIII.		If the aircraft is redesigned with simplified structure then two aircraft can be built instead of one ; with the new radial engine of increased power the loss in performance is only of the order of 5 m.p.h.

The evolution of a bomber design during the Second World War: a not-too-serious view by G.H. Forster.

of the Ju 88A-1 was 40 pounds. By the mid-war period the Mosquito was up to 50 pounds, the Messerschmitt 410 to 54 pounds and the B-26 Marauder stood at 56 pounds. By the end of the conflict the German Arado 234 was loaded to 76 pounds for take-off and the B-29 was loaded to 77 pounds. The German Junkers 86R, the only truly high altitude bomber to be used operationally during the war, sidestepped this trend. For flights at 42,000 feet and above, its huge wing, with a span slightly greater than that of the B-17 and pointed at the tips to reduce drag due to vortices at high altitude, was loaded to only 24 pounds per square foot.

Another tendency during the war was for wings to have progressively higher aspect ratios; in other words, they became longer and narrower for a given area. By raising the aspect ratio designers could reduce the induced drag (the drag caused by producing lift to keep the aircraft in the air). For the shorter range flights the reduction in drag from a high aspect ratio wing did not compensate for its higher structural weight; over the longer ranges, however, the fuel saved by employing such a wing soon made up for its disadvantages.

Aerodynamically, too, bombers continued to get much cleaner. By the end of the war the large drag-producing manned gun turret was on the way out except for tail positions where they could be streamlined; in their place came the smaller remotely controlled barbettes for the guns.

The tendency for aerodynamically cleaner bombers with higher wing loadings to land faster, led to the increased importance of braking systems to stop aircraft within reasonable distances. In effect brakes make it difficult for wheels to rotate relative to the fixed undercarriage legs, and over-fierce braking will cause an aircraft with a conventional tail-wheel undercarriage to tip on to its nose. To overcome this problem designers moved the main undercarriage legs further forward of the aircraft's centre of gravity. But this in its turn placed a greater proportion of the weight on to

The first four-engined bomber of modern design to see action during the war was the German Focke Wulf 200 Kondor. Developed from the design of an airliner, the FW 200C was powered by four 1,200 horse power Bramo 323 radials and had a maximum speed of 224 mph; carrying 2,000 pounds of bombs, it had an effective operational radius of about 850 miles.

Although it had a good range performance which made it suitable for anti-shipping operations, the weak structure of the Kondor was easily over-stressed in combat and from time to time aircraft broke their backs following heavy landings.

A Short Stirling, showing off its Gouge-type flaps; as well as increasing the lift coefficient of the wing when they were extended, these flaps increased the wing area by about a quarter. The first modern purpose-built four-engined bomber to go into action during the war, the Stirling I was powered by four 1,590 horse power Bristol Hercules engines and had a maximum speed of 270 mph; carrying 2,000 pounds of bombs, it had an effective operational radius of about 1,000 miles, or with 14,000 pounds of bombs its radius was about 250 miles.

Armourers loading 500 pound bombs into a Stirling. The Stirling's internal bomb bay was greater in area than that of any other wartime bomber: the main bay under the fuselage was 42 feet long and three feet wide; there was a further stowage for bombs in each of the wing inboard sections. *C. Brown*

The Martin B-26 Marauder, showing off its clean lines from an unusual aspect. This aircraft was powered by two 2,000 horse power Pratt and Whitney Double Wasp radials and had a maximum speed of 282 mph; carrying 2,000 pounds of bombs, it had an effective operational radius of about 550 miles. *C. Brown*

The Petlyakov Pe-8 was the only modern Russian heavy bomber type to see action during the war; and less than eighty were built. Powered by four 1,350 horse power AM 35A engines, it had a maximum speed of 273 mph; carrying 2,000 pounds of bombs, its effective operational radius was about 900 miles. *IWM*

Units equipped with the B-17 Fortress formed the backbone of the US heavy bomber force in Europe during the war. The B-17G, depicted, was powered by four 1,200 horse power/turbo-supercharged radials and had a maximum speed of 302 mph. Carrying 2,000 pounds of bombs, it had an effective operational radius of about 950 miles. *USAF*

The Il'yushin Il-4 was the most-used Russian medium range bomber during the war. Powered by two 1,100 horse power M-88 radials, it had a maximum speed of 267 mph; carrying 2,000 pounds of bombs, it had an effective operational radius of about 450 miles.

The Mitsubishi G4M (Allied code-name 'Betty') replaced the G3M in many Japanese Navy bomber units. Like the earlier bomber, the G4M initially carried no armour or self-sealing tanks; later versions carried self-sealing fuel tanks but to the end there was only minimal armour protection. The G4M2, depicted, was powered by two 1,800 horse power Kasei engines and had a maximum speed of 272 mph; carrying 2,000 pounds of bombs, its effective operational radius was about 1,500 miles. *Selinger*

Layout of the Boeing B-17G Fortress.

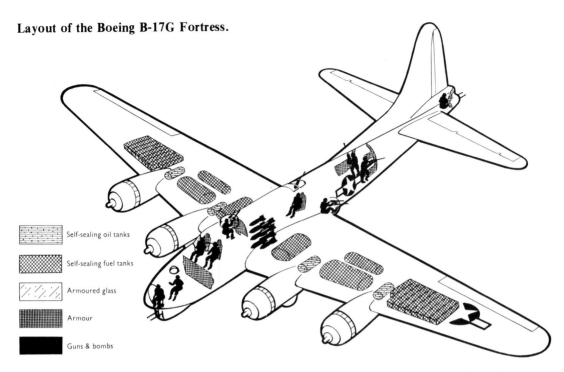

Self-sealing oil tanks

Self-sealing fuel tanks

Armoured glass

Armour

Guns & bombs

the tail wheel and both it and the fuselage had to be strengthened to take the increased load; it also increased the tendency of the aircraft to become unstable and ground-loop during landing. The real answer was the nose-wheel undercarriage, and by the end of the war most new bomber types were fitted with it. Compared with a tail-wheel undercarriage for an aircraft of similar weight, a nose-wheel undercarriage was about 10 per cent heavier; but the latter's advantages greatly outweighed its disadvantages.

With a single exception, during the Second World War bombers did not get much larger, externally, than the early B-17 with its wing span of 103 feet 9 inches. The exception was the Boeing B-29, a bomber as much in a class of its own in 1945 as the B-17 had been in 1939. In its aerodynamic conception the B-29 was competent rather than clever; there was no attempt to push the 'state of the art' further than it was known it would go. With a span of just over 141 feet, the B-29's wing was about 40 per cent longer than that of the B-17. At its maximum take-off weight of 135,000 pounds the B-29 was more than three times as heavy as

the B-17A of 1939; and it was twice as heavy as the B-17G of 1943 and the B-24 Liberator, Lancaster, Halifax and Heinkel 177 bombers which were in the next weight bracket. Attacking targets up to 1,100 miles from its base the B-29B, a version stripped of much of its defensive armament and used for night attacks, could carry a maximum bomb load of 22,800 pounds — *equal to the weight of a fully laden Junkers 88A-1*. The B-29 was indeed a superb technical achievement and it represented the pinnacle of bomber design during the Second World War.

The Performance of the Bomber

Before going any further, it might be as well to examine the figures issued for the performance of bombers during the Second World War. Makers' figures for terms such as maximum speed, cruising speed, a maximum bomb load and range are often bandied about as though they really bore a relation to the operational capability of the aircraft being described. Alas, this is not the case. The

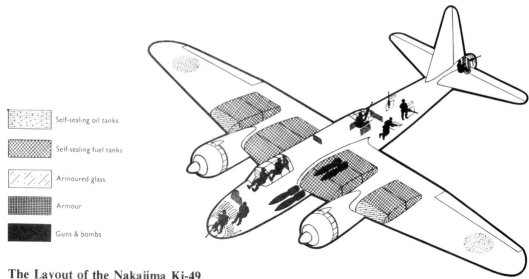

Self-sealing oil tanks

Self-sealing fuel tanks

Armoured glass

Armour

Guns & bombs

The Layout of the Nakajima Ki-49

(Allied code-name 'Helen'), showing that when
they put their minds to it the Japanese would
armour their bombers as extensively as anyone
else.

The main production version of th Ki-49 was
powered by two 1,500 horse power Nakajima Ha-
109 radials and had a maximum speed of 306 mph;
carrying 2,000 pounds of bombs, its effective radius
of action was 700 miles. *Selinger*

maximum speed usually given, for example, is
that which an unladen aircraft can attain for a
short time. If a bomber aircraft can be likened
to a cart horse, a fair analogy to maximum
speed would be the rate at which a randy punch
could dash the length of a small field after a
mare on heat; of academic interest and good for
a snigger, perhaps, but hardly indicative of the
horse's ability to draw a useful load anywhere.

The Douglas A-26 Invader attack bomber, which became operational late in 1944, showing off its high aspect ratio wing, upper gun barbette and generally clean lines. Powered by two 2,000 horse power Pratt and Whitney Double Wasp radials, it had a maximum speed of 355 mph; carrying 2,000 pounds of bombs, it had an effective operational radius of about 600 miles. *Douglas*

For the average bomber crew flight at maximum speed was an extremely expensive luxury, for it boosted fuel consumption to two or even three times that at economical cruising revolutions. In the same way, figures for cruising speed, bomb load and range are meaningless unless all are carefully related and the aircraft was carrying all of its military equipment and a full crew (*obviously* an aircraft can fly faster and further if the guns are not loaded and half of the crew stay on the ground).

To be charitable, it must be said that aircraft manufacturers have to sell aircraft just as car manufacturers have to sell cars. And while rarely will either stoop to telling downright lies about their products, they will often fail to reveal the full unvarnished truth.

So now let us take a close look at the figures for one Second World War bomber, the B-29.

And before the Boeing company begins a libel action to deprive me of every penny I own, I must make it clear that I have chosen this aircraft because it was able to carry heavy loads further than any other and so the intricate balance between fuel requirements and bomb loads can best be shown. I do not wish to imply that Boeing's figures are any more misleading than those from any other manufacturer. The figures usually quoted for the B-29 are: maximum speed 357 mph; maximum cruising speed 342 mph; economical cruising speed 220 mph; maximum bomb load 20,000 pounds; and practical bomb load 5,000 pounds over a range of 3,250 miles. How realistic a picture do these figures convey of the bomber's actual operational capability?

To find out, let us examine in some detail the fuel and bomb load calculations for a typical operational mission by a B-29, against a target

1,730 miles away from its base (to simplify the discussion we shall omit the effects of wind, though this would of course have to be taken into account in any actual calculations). In our example the target has to be attacked from 20,000 feet, and to penetrate the defences the aircraft must be at this altitude for sixty miles either side of the target.

The maximum take-off weight of the B-29 was 135,000 pounds. To find the weight of bombs that could be carried to the target on this mission, we must first look at the weight of the aircraft when it landed back at base afterwards. To allow some flexibility in case the airfield was not usable when it got back, an endurance reserve of 3,000 pounds of fuel was to be carried*. If an engine failed the remaining three would have had to work harder to take the bomber home, so to allow for this possibility a three-engine reserve of 2,610 pounds had also to be carried. So, if things did not get too rough and everything went according to plan, the B-29 should return to base weighing 88,000 pounds made up as follows:

Basic weight	75,890 pounds
Crew, 11 men	2,200 pounds
Bomb racks and shackles	800 pounds
Oil	2,250 pounds
Ammunition, 3,000 rounds	900 pounds
Reserve fuel	5,610 pounds
Landing and taxying fuel	350 pounds

Allowing twenty minutes engine running for warm up and taxying, the bomber would burn 500 pounds of fuel before it started its take-off run. The take-off of the heavily laden aircraft would take about two minutes before it was established on course for the target, and would consume a further 240 pounds of fuel. Thus, by the time the bomber was actually airborne and pointing in the right direction, there would be 740 pounds of fuel less for the flight.

The take-off weight of 135,000 pounds, less 88,740 pounds landing weight plus take-off

*In this section fuel is measured in pounds, to make the calculations easier. An Imperial gallon of aviation fuel weighs 7.2 pounds, a US gallon weighs 5.9 pounds.

allowances, left 46,260 pounds to be split between fuel and bombs. In the case of our B-29 it was worked out that the total fuel requirement for the mission, excluding reserves, was 34,907 pounds. This left 12,433 pounds for bombs; but it was a requirement that our target had to be attacked with 1,000 pound bombs, so only twelve of these could be carried.

Let us now follow the bomber through its mission. The take-off was normal and the B-29 covered 34 miles during its climb at just over 450 feet per minute, to 5,000 feet. There it levelled off. The crew could have continued their climb straight to 20,000 feet but the bomber was still very heavy; during its climb so far it had been burning 30 pounds of fuel for each mile covered. The easy passage through the rarefied air at 20,000 feet would not have made up for the amount of fuel burned getting the heavy bomber up there. To save fuel it was decided to delay the climb to 20,000 feet until as late as possible; by then a great deal of fuel would have been burned and the B-29 would be much lighter. The flight engineer eased back the throttles and the bomber droned towards its target at 205 mph, burning only 11 pounds of fuel per mile.

The 5,000 foot cruise lasted for almost seven hours during which the bomber covered 1,530 miles. During this time it burned 16,240 pounds of fuel and by the end of it the engineer had throttled back until the consumption was down to 10 pounds per mile. Now, however, 166 miles from the target, the climb had to begin to penetrate the defences at 20,000 feet. The engineer increased power and the bomber began its climb at 550 feet per minute. This second climb took 27 minutes and covered 106 miles, burning 23 pounds of fuel per mile.

When it levelled off at 20,000 feet the B-29 had a true airspeed of 260 mph for its dart to the target; its weight now down to 114,500 pounds, the bomber slid smoothly through the rarefied air burning 11 pounds of fuel per mile. At the target the 12,000 pounds of bombs were shed and fuel consumption dropped to 10 pounds per mile. Once the bomber was the mandatory 60 miles from the target the engineer reduced

The magnificent Boeing B-29 Superfortress, the type which marked the zenith of heavy bomber design in 1945 and whose performance is described in detail in the text. Powered by four 2,200 horse power Wright Cyclone 18 turbo-supercharged radials, it had a maximum speed of 357 mph.
Boeing

power and the B-29 began to slow descent at 200 feet per minute; the aircraft covered the next 100 miles at 240 mph burning only 8 pounds per mile.

At 15,000 feet the bomber levelled off yet again, for the main part of the cruise home. This lasted just over five and a half hours and covered 1,330 miles at an average of 7.8 pounds of fuel per mile. By the end of this time the bomber's weight was down to 90,000 pounds and home was 240 miles away. The engineer throttled back yet again and the aircraft descended at 200 feet per minute for the next hour and ten minutes, burning 6.6 pounds per mile. Fifteen hours and 28 minutes after take-off, tired, hungry and with sore backsides, our heroes landed back at base. Their B-29 had covered the 3,460 mile round trip at an overall average speed of 224 mph.

Now we can see how misleading are the usually quoted figures for the B-29. One of these bombers carrying no bombs and hardly

any fuel probably could scream along at 357 mph for a short time and 342 mph for a little longer; but so what?

Generally speaking, piston-engined bombers performed most efficiently (that is to say they were able to transport the greatest bomb load to a given target) when they were flown at their optimum range speeds; the latter was usually about two thirds of the aircraft's maximum speed at a given altitude. During the course of the war there was a slight but not a great increase in the speeds at which piston-engined bombers attacked from high level, except for the high-speed unarmed types attacking by day. As the ground anti-aircraft defences steadily improved, however, bombers were forced to use their extra performance to fly progressively higher to avoid the effects of the gunfire; attack altitudes for horizontal bombers increased from around 10,000 feet at the beginning of the war, to between 20,000 and 30,000 feet at the end. For low-level attacks it was a different matter: light Flak was so effective that high attacking speeds were necessary, even though it meant consuming additional fuel that had to be carried in place of part of the bomb load.

The characteristics of the jet engine were quite different to those of the piston engine, and as a result jet aircraft performed quite

Interior of the nose of the B-29, showing the pilot's
and co-pilot's controls on the left and right
respectively. In the centre is the bombardier/nose
gunner's position with the Norden bombsight; the
nose gunsight, with the controls for the upper and
lower forward gun barbettes, is folded out of the
way and is just visible above the co-pilot's
instrument panel. *Boeing*

differently. The jet was at its most efficient
when it was running at maximum thrust at high
altitude. As a result the German Me 262 and Ar
234 jet bombers cruised at speeds close to their
maxima during operational missions. At
33,000 feet the Jumo 004 fitted to these aircraft
consumed only one third the fuel required for
the same thrust at sea level.

The Structure of the Bomber

From the time it was first introduced into
aircraft, the all-metal stressed skin method of
construction demonstrated a clear advantage
over the older methods using fabric to cover a
simple metal or wooden framework. For a
given weight an all-metal structure was both
stronger and stiffer. Moreover, since metal
panels could be beaten into almost any shape, it
was easier to fashion them to conform with the
latest demands of streamlining.

As bomber structures steadily became larger
and heavier, skill and ingenuity in design paid
far greater dividends than had been the case
earlier; and, as more was learned about the
stressing of aircraft, structures became more
efficient. Simultaneously there was a gradual
improvement in the materials available for the
construction of aircraft: during the decade
between 1935 and 1945 the strength-to-weight
ratio of the light alloys in use increased by
about one quarter. This improvement was
achieved by alloying small amounts of zinc and
copper, in differing proportions, with the basic
aluminium. As a result of these progressive
changes, the structures of bomber types
entering service at the end of the war were
considerably more efficient than those at the
beginning.

Stressed skin all-metal construction saw
almost universal use for bombers. There were,

however, a couple of successful designs in
Britain which employed quite different
methods: the Vickers Wellington and the de
Havilland Mosquito.

The Wellington was constructed using the

Although it produced a strong structure able to
survive quite appalling battle damage, as in the
case of this Wellington which returned after
suffering a near direct-hit from a heavy Flak shell,
the geodetic method of construction was not taken
up by other aircraft manufacturers. *IWM*

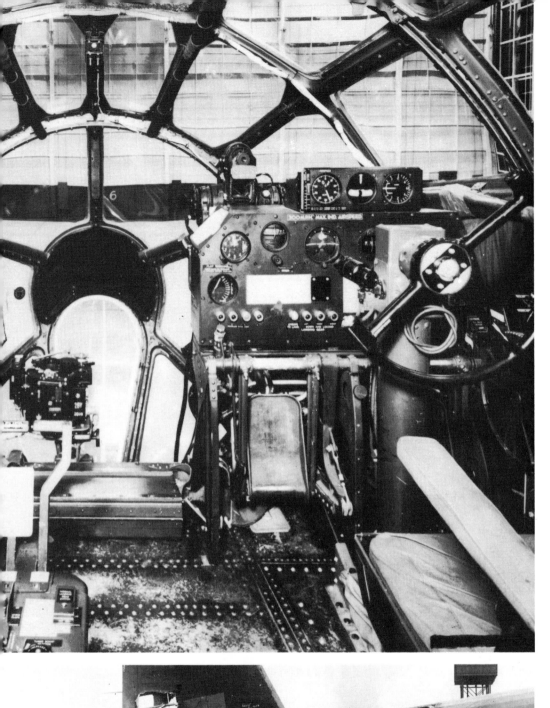

so-called geodetic method; a geodetic is the curve taken by a string stretched over a curved surface, and the structure of the Wellington was formed out of such geodetics of metal in the shape of the fuselage and the wings. The resultant basket-like form was covered with fabric. One advantage of this method was that it had a considerable reserve of strength, which enabled Wellingtons to return home with quite appalling battle damage. This form of construction did, however, have its drawbacks. Production was difficult and involved somewhat more man-hours than a similar all-metal bomber. And although geodetic methods were good for building continuous structures, an aircraft did not come into that category. Great holes had to be cut into the structure for gun turrets, to bury wheels after retraction and

to get men and bombs in and out of the aircraft; these holes had to be surrounded by hefty frames loaded at the points where the geodetics happened to meet them and this added greatly to the overall weight of the structure. Whether the advantages of the geodetic system made up for its disadvantages is open to some doubt; significantly, nobody else bothered to jump on that particular bandwagon.

The other successful bomber not to employ all-metal construction was the Mosquito, whose structure was almost entirely of wood. The use of wood in the construction of aircraft conferred two great advantages which would not be considered except in time of war: first, it enabled aircraft to be built without using the light alloys which were likely to be in short supply; and secondly, it enabled the woodworking industry to take part in the production of aircraft at a time when the metalworking industry was over-extended. That said, it has to be admitted that for a

The wooden Mosquito demonstrated that it, too, could survive considerable punishment. This aircraft was hit by Flak during an attack on a V1 launching site early in 1944. *IWM*

bomber with an all-up weight of about 20,000 pounds wood made an ideal material. Before the war the de Havilland company gained a great deal of experience working with it and by 1940 had developed its use to a fine art. In the case of the Mosquito the fuselage shell was made in two halves, each built up in layers using plywood round a thick central core of balsa wood and glued under pressure in a shaped mould. The wing was built up round two spruce box-spars, with spruce and plywood ribs and a skin of plywood. The result was a highly efficient structure that was both strong and stiff. Since the joints were glued, an extremely smooth exterior was possible with no rivet heads to worry about. There was the disadvantage that a wooden structure did not weather so well as a metal one; but in wartime it was rare for a bomber to survive to the end of its structural life.

Whatever the method of construction, bomber structures were normally stressed to take about 4g, in the case of heavy bombers like

the Lancaster and the B-17, and about 8g in the case of medium bombers like the Junkers 88 and the Mosquito. Just before the war the Germans became hooked on dive-bombing as a method of attack and the Luftwaffe issued a requirement that all of its new bombers should be able to attack in dives of at least 60 degrees. From the point of view of bombing accuracy at the time, the idea had a lot to commend it; but it gave nightmares to the German structures people. The dive itself presented few problems; but at some stage the aircraft had to pull out of it and that meant that the structure had to be able to withstand about 6g. This was not too bad for smaller bombers like the Ju 88 which had been stressed above this figure anyway. But when Dornier tried to make their 30,000-pound Do 217 do it they had no end of trouble. And when Heinkel tried to do the same thing with their 60,000 pound He 177 the result was a fiasco. The weight of the bombers' structures went up almost in direct proportion to the amount of extra strength required, with the

Built in its initial production versions as a dive bomber, the thirty-ton Heinkel 177 was far too heavy for this task. Although it had the appearance of a twin-engined bomber, the He 177 had two coupled engines driving each airscrew (see page 54). The He 177A-3, depicted, had a maximum speed of 303 mph and carrying 2,000 pounds of bombs it had an effective operational radius of about 1,200 miles. *Redemann*

result that both aircraft put on a lot of weight during their design stages — though usually not enough to enable them to pull out of their dives later without popping some rivets and sometimes wrinkling the skin. Fortunately for the Luftwaffe, the Zeiss company came up with a type of bombsight which made accurate horizontal attacks possible (see page 76); with a sigh of relief all round, the requirement was dropped that such heavy aircraft should be able to dive-bomb.

By the beginning of the 1940s operational bomber types were able to reach altitudes above 35,000 feet, which was close to the limits even for a man breathing pure oxygen. For fighter pilots the problem was not serious because they were never up there for long. But for bomber crews the longer periods at high altitude meant a greater chance of decompression sickness in one or more of its gruesome forms: the bends, a dull ache in the joints; the creeps, an itching feeling; or the chokes, a constricting pain across the chest. The answer to the problem was an airtight pressurized cabin, which would provide the

crew with an environment similar to that lower down.

The first bomber to become operational with a pressurized cabin was the German Junkers 86R, which carried out attacks on targets in southern England in the summer of 1942. The two-man crew was ensconced in a small cabin which, at altitudes around 45,000 feet, had a pressure differential of about 8 pounds per square inch above the outside air; it was sufficient to allow the men to breath normally without oxygen masks. To prevent the cabin exploding like a toy balloon if it was holed by enemy fire, the crew had to depressurize if they came under attack and re-pressurize afterwards.

In the spring of 1944 the Mosquito Mark XVI entered service with a pressurized cabin rather less ambitious than that of the Ju 86. It provided a pressure differential of only 2 psi, which meant that the crew still had to wear their oxygen masks but they were treated to a more comfortable ride than would otherwise have been the case.

The B-29, which entered service in the

The Junkers 86R was the only truly stratospheric bomber to go into action during the war; in the summer of 1942 a few of them carried out attacks on targets in southern England from altitudes of over 40,000 feet. This aircraft was also the first bomber type to go into action fitted with a pressurized cabin. The Ju 86R was powered by two

1,000 horse power Jumo 207B turbo-supercharged diesel engines and had a maximum speed at operational altitude of 205 mph; carrying its maximum bomb load for high altitude attacks of 550 pounds, it had an effective operational radius of about 200 miles.

summer of 1944, showed that the pressurized cabin had really come to stay. This remarkable bomber carried three such cabins: in the nose, in the centre fuselage and one in the tail for the gunner; the nose and centre cabins were joined by a pressurized tunnel. The 6.5 psi pressure differential held the cabins to the equivalent of 8,000 feet when the aircraft was at 30,000 feet. The 8,000 foot pressure equivalent was important because it meant that by day oxygen masks did not have to be worn and in-flight fatigue was greatly reduced. By night the pilots and gunners had to be on oxygen if the cabin altitude was above 4,000 feet, if they were to retain their full night vision capability.

Except when they were attacking targets very close to their bases, bombers took off carrying fuel loads far heavier than their bomb loads. Most or all of the fuel was housed in the wings, an efficient place to carry such a load since the supporting lift was generated directly under the weight. To minimise the loss if a tank was holed, bombers carried their fuel in several separate tanks.

During the course of the war self-sealing fuel tanks became a standard fitting to bombers of all nations. In addition, some Russian and Japanese bombers carried systems to pipe exhaust gases or carbon dioxide into the fuel tanks. By thus substituting inert gases for the potentially explosive fuel-air mixture in partially empty or empty tanks, the risk of explosion was reduced.

After the early war period, most bombers carried a measure of armour protection for the pilot and favoured crew members. The amount of armour that could be carried was always limited, however, and reduced the aircraft's range or load-carrying ability.

When a bomber returned from raids with pieces shot off or holes in the structure, the aircraft had to be repaired before it could go into action again. The number of bombers available for the next attack was critically dependent upon the speed with which the damage could be made good and rapid repair was vitally important. In the case of the Lancaster bomber, for example, about 1,000 pounds of the structural weight was taken up in bolts and flanges for rapid dismantling; in other words, had it been constructed in one piece it could have carried 1,000 pounds more bombs over a given range, or flown faster or higher. But this extra lifting capacity or performance would have been dearly bought in terms of the time aircraft were forced to remain on the ground for repairs.

One of the most detailed sources of information on the effects of different types of damage to bombers is a US Navy survey conducted in the Pacific between September 1944 and August 1945. A total of 354 cases in which PB4Y Liberator bombers were lost or damaged by enemy action were recorded and the results were as follows:

Position of Hit	Total Number of Aircraft Hit	Number of Aircraft Lost	Percentage Loss of Aircraft Hit
Propeller	7	0	0
Power plant	57	21	37
Structure	135	5	4
Pilot and/or controls	29	6	20
Control surfaces	20	0	0
Oil system	9	3	33
Fuel system	31	8	26
Hydraulic system	17	2	12
Electrical system	9	1	11
Others	40	0	0
	354	46	13

This B-17 returned home with its fuselage blown open by a Flak shell exploding nearby. *USAF*

In the survey a lost aircraft was defined as one that had failed to return to a friendly base after being hit; a damaged aircraft was one that had returned to base after being hit, whether it was repairable or not. Like all American bombers, the Liberator was powered by air-cooled engines; had it been fitted with liquid-cooled engines, a greater number would have been lost to hits in this area. In general terms, liquid-cooled engines were twice as vulnerable to enemy action as are those with air-cooling.

Several interesting points emerge from the table. For heavy bombers the greatest single cause of loss was hits to the engines, though there was a 63 per cent chance of returning with

Rammed by a Russian fighter while attacking shipping off the Crimea in August 1941, this Junkers 88 of Kampfgeschwader 51 lost the whole of the starboard side of the tailplane and had the fin and port tailplane twisted through about 20 degrees. The pilot succeeded in flying the aircraft in this condition for about 100 miles to friendly territory, before the tail finally broke away; the crew parachuted safely to earth. *Dierich*

During the war bombers frequently demonstrated that they could remain airborne with quite major damage to their structures. Fires, however, once they reached the fuel, were almost invariably lethal. In this photograph a B-26 Marauder is seen in its final moments, after being hit by Flak over Germany early in 1945. *USAF*

such damage. Next in vulnerability were the hydraulic, fuel and oil systems, with 88, 74 and 67 per cent chances of survival, respectively; where aircraft were lost to these causes, it was generally the result of a fuel or oil fire (in a similar survey into heavy bomber losses carried out by the US Army Air Force, fire was present in half of those lost). The pilot and the controls constituted another vulnerable area, but they were a small target and only 13 per cent of the bombers in the sample were lost to hits in this area. The other parts of the bomber were shown to be relatively invulnerable to enemy action.

The Power to Strike

The story of the evolution of the aero engine during the Second World War has been covered in some detail in *World War II Fighter Conflict*. Since in all nations the same types of engine were used to power both bombers and fighters, it is not intended to repeat the description in this book. Fighter engines were required to provide maximum power in short bursts, whereas those of bombers had to be able to plod along for many hours at cruising revolutions. These differences were not so irreconcilable, however, as to justify the development of separate types of engine for each.

That said, there were one or two developments in motors used only to power bombers, which justify mention in this section. Before the war there were attempts to get twice as much power out of engines already in existence, by the seemingly simple expedient of joining two of them together. Three such double engines went into service: the British Rolls-Royce Vulture and the German Daimler Benz 606 and 610 designs. None was successful.

As a basis for the Vulture, Rolls-Royce took the Kestrel, its successful 715 horse power V-12 with a capacity of 21 litres. The idea was to use the basic cylinder arrangement of two Kestrels,

Ground crewmen working on the Wright Cyclone 9
radials of a B-17 Fortress. These units developed
1,200 horse power each at sea level and, boosted by
the exhaust-driven turbo-superchargers, 1,000
horse power at 25,000 feet. *C. Brown*

The Rolls-Royce Vulture, a 24 cylinder engine of
'X' layout, developed 1,845 horse power for the
Avro Manchester. The engine lacked development
potential, however, and was soon dropped.

The Daimler Benz 610 was a double engine, made
up of two 1,475 horse power DB 605s mounted
side-by-side and driving a single airscrew through a
common reduction gear. Fitted to the later versions
of the Heinkel 177, the DB 610 gave continual
troubles which were not sorted out before the
demise of the German heavy bomber force. *IWM*

one inverted under the other, to form a 24 cylinder 42 litre engine of X-layout with all the pistons connected to a common crank shaft. The Vulture developed 1,845 horse power and went into production early in 1940 for the twin-engined Avro Manchester bomber, but soon ran into trouble. Quite apart from suffering the teething troubles to be expected with any new engine, it soon became clear that it would not be easy to develop the Vulture to get much more power out of it. And in wartime engine development was all-important, because there simply was not the time to introduce new designs whenever extra power was needed. Meanwhile, Rolls-Royce's Merlin was steadily rising in power and it was performing successfully in the four-engined Halifax bomber. The Royal Air Force was forced to take a more serious look at Avro's proposal for a Manchester with a wing re-designed to take four Merlins. The result was the Lancaster, one of the war's most successful bombers. The Vulture was quietly dropped.

Working independently in Germany, Daimler Benz tried a similar short cut, with unfortunate results. Just before the war the Heinkel company badly wanted a 2,500 horse power engine for the new He 177 heavy bomber. At the time no such engine was available in Germany so Daimler Benz took a pair of its proven DB 601s (the same $\wedge$ -12 engine that powered the Messerschmitt 109 fighter), mounted them side-by-side in an '$\wedge\wedge$' arrangement with a gear box on the front driving a common airscrew shaft, and called it the DB 606. The pilot was provided with a system to enable him to declutch either engine from the propeller shaft, so that failure of one did not preclude the use of the other. The 67.8 litre Siamese-twin developed 2,700 horse power for take-off. But then the troubles began.

Between them Daimler Benz and Heinkel had tried to be a little bit too clever and the engine installation provided lots of excitement for those who flew the He 177. The DB 606 was difficult to maintain; moreover lubrication was inadequate and the engine was liable to seize up if the throttles were not handled carefully, and there were frequent engine fires caused by fuel leaking from injectors.

One would have thought that the DB 606 would have shown everyone that the Siamese-twin arrangement for engines was not really a short cut. But by mid-1942 the Luftwaffe was screaming for its new heavy bomber; the He 177 had made its first flight at about the same time as the British Halifax, which by then had been in service for over a year. Instead of ditching the DB 606 and putting in four DB 601s, solving the problem as Avro had with the Lancaster, it was decided to re-engine the bomber with the DB 610 — a double engine made up of two DB 605s. This 71.4 litre engine gave just under 3,000 horse power for take-off; but many of the old problems remained and the engine required careful handling. The Heinkel 177 did not become operational as a bomber until the summer of 1943; and the engine's problems had not been fully resolved a year later, when the fuel famine due to the successful Allied attacks on the German oil industry put an effective end to heavy bomber operations by the Luftwaffe.

With but a single exception, the piston engines which powered bombers on operations during the Second World War were all of the conventional four-stroke spark ignition type. The exception was the German Jumo 207B, a two-stroke compression ignition diesel fitted into the Junkers 86R high altitude bomber. Amongst the points of technical interest in this 16.6 litre engine was the fact that it employed two reciprocating pistons in each of the six cylinders.

The attraction of the diesel was that its far higher compression ratio, about two and a half times that of a high powered petrol engine, extracted greater energy from a given amount of fuel and so consumed less for a given power; power for power, a diesel engine burned about a fifth less fuel than a conventional engine. And, as we have observed repeatedly, if fuel consumption can be reduced range or bomb load can be increased. There were, of course, penalties to pay for this advantage: the higher compression ratio necessitated an engine which was stronger all round and which was much heavier. A diesel weighed nearly twice as much as a petrol engine developing the same power.

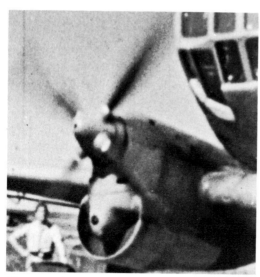

Close-up of the Jumo 207B installation of the
Junkers 86R high altitude bomber. This engine was
fitted with a turbo-supercharger for first-stage
boosting, and a mechanically-driven second-stage
supercharger; in addition, to further improve high
altitude performance, nitrous oxide was injected
into the second-stage supercharger to cool the
charge and provide additional oxygen for
combustion. *Goetz*

The first jet aircraft to undertake bombing
operations was the Messerschmitt 262, a converted
fighter. The German bomber unit
Kampfgeschwader 51, two of whose aircraft are
depicted, began operations with Me 262s in July
1944 against targets in the Normandy bridgehead
area. On the nearer aircraft two 551-pound bombs
are visible, mounted externally under the nose.
Although it had a top speed of about 500 mph
when carrying bombs and 540 mph 'clean' the short
radius of action at low altitude and the lack of a
suitable bomb sight for high altitude horizontal
attacks prevented the type from being successful in
this role. *Dierich*

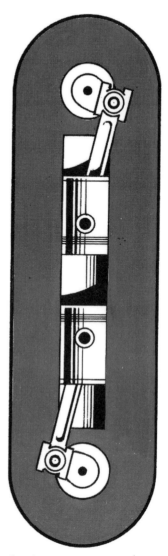

Diagram showing the layout of the reciprocating
pistons of the Jumo 207B compression ignition
diesel engine; the engine was a liquid-cooled in-
line, with six such cylinders.

With a pair of bombs mounted externally and just visible under the engine nacelles, an Arado 234 of *Kampfgeschwader 76* is seen trailing smoke as it gets airborne under the combined thrust of two 1,984-pound thrust Jumo 004B jet engines augmented by two 1,100-pound thrust Walther 109-500 rocket pods. The Arado 234 was the first true bomber type to go into service powered by jet engines. Carrying two 1,100-pound bombs, its maximum speed was 420 mph, rising to 457 mph after the bombs had been released; with this load it had an effective operational radius of about 300 miles at high altitude. *KG 76 Archive*

Since the 1920s the Junkers company had been dabbling with diesels for aircraft, but even for long range aircraft the overall advantages of this form of power plant were not great. There were other reasons for fitting the Jumo 207B to the Junkers 86R. The Jumo 207B developed 1,000 horse power for take-off and with two stage supercharging (the first stage a turbo-supercharger driven by the exhaust gases) and nitrous oxide injection it gave 750 horse power at 40,000 feet. On a pair of these engines the

A straddling ground-crewman lends scale to the small frontal area of the Jumo 004B installed in an Arado 234; this engine had a diameter of just over 31 inches. *KG 76 Archive*

Junkers 86R carried out bombing operations
from altitudes up to 43,000 feet. The diesel
engine is not intrinsically superior to the petrol
engine for high altitude operations; but its
exhaust gases emerge at a temperature
somewhat lower than those from a petrol
engine, which allowed the struggling German
turbo-supercharger technology (which lagged
far behind that of the Americans) to cope with
the problems involved.

Two types of jet aircraft went into service
with bomber units during the Second World
War, both with the Luftwaffe: the
Messerschmitt 262 and the Arado 234. Both
aircraft were powered by the Jumo 004B which
developed just under 2,000 pounds of thrust for
take-off. This engine has been described in
some detail in *World War II Fighter Conflict*.

Most nations played with the idea of using
simple powder rockets to assist heavily laden
aircraft to get airborne; but only rarely was this
form of boosting used for operational missions.
One problem was that the powder rockets were
not all that reliable. If there was a failure on
take-off, the pilot could find himself roaring
down the runway with somewhat less thrust
than was necessary to get the overladen aircraft
airborne. The experience could take years off a
man's life.

Only in Germany was a reliable rocket

Groundcrewmen loading a Walther 109-500
rocket pod on to an Arado 234. Complete with
hydrogen peroxide and sodium permanganate for
30 seconds' running, the pod weighed just over 600
pounds; on the front of the pod can be seen the bag
for the parachute. *Goetz*

booster developed and used for normal operations. The unit was the Walther 109-500, comprising a 1,100 pound thrust liquid-fuel rocket neatly enclosed in a streamlined pod; complete with sufficient hydrogen peroxide and sodium permanganate for 30 seconds' running at full thrust, the pod weighed just over 600 pounds. Once the fuel was exhausted the pilot jettisoned the pods, which descended by parachute and could be re-used. For the Arado 234s, laden with bombs and powered by primitive jet engines which gave poor acceleration, the extra 2,200 pounds of thrust from a pair of Walther rockets made all the difference when it came to getting off short runways.

Defending the Bomber

The type of defensive gun position fitted to most bombers at the beginning of the war was the simple hand-held machine gun pivoting on a mounting fixed to the aircraft structure. Operationally, this type of mounting was soon found to have severe disadvantages: since there was a limit to what the gunner's muscle power could aim against a 200 mph slipstream, only one gun could be handled on such a mounting in any but the fore or aft position; and the field of fire was always limited. Such gun positions could be either open or enclosed, but if the latter the field of fire was further reduced.

The next stage was to provide the gunner with a rotatable mounting, so that he could swing the pivot and therefore the gun to align it approximately on the fighter and make the fine corrections by hand. This made things somewhat easier and, since the gun could now be swung round the gunner instead of round the fixed pivot, the field of fire was greatly increased.

The old problem of the gunner having to battle with the slipstream, when engaging targets to the side, still remained; but in the gun positions fitted to some Italian bombers this difficulty was overcome in a rather clever manner. On the CANT Z1007, for example, the enclosed hand-operated dorsal position housed a 12.7mm gun. The turret was operated by an inverted control column with a wheel at the lower end; rotation of the wheel rotated the gun turret, while movement of the column towards or away from the gunner elevated or depressed the gun. A light alloy tube projected through the turret on the side opposite to the gun, but was geared to the gun so that it elevated with it

A manually-operated rotatable mounting, as fitted in the open dorsal gun position of the Focke Wulf Kondor; the weapon was a 13 mm Rheinmetall-Borsig MG 131 machine gun. *Jope*

The simplest type of defensive gun position was the hand-held machine gun pivoting on a mounting fixed to the aircraft structure: depicted are machine gunners in the waist position of a B-17 Fortress, with .5-in Browning guns. *USAF*

The CANT Z 1007bis, showing the manual dorsal turret fitted to several Italian bomber types. Acting as an aerodynamic balance for the 12.7 mm Breda machine gun was a light alloy tube, which projected through the opposite side of the turret and elevated with the gun. On the power of three 1,000 horse power Piaggio P XI engines, this bomber had a maximum speed of 280 mph; carrying 2,000 pounds of bombs, it had an effective operational radius of about 500 miles. *via Ghiselli*

and so acted as an aerodynamic balance. It was a neat way to overcome the slipstream forces, but long before it entered service it had been overtaken by the greatly superior power-driven systems.

The simplest form of powered gun turret employed an electric motor to traverse the turret and the gun mounting ring, with the gunner doing the fine laying in azimuth and elevation by hand. Typical of these systems was the DL 131 turret fitted in the dorsal position of the Dornier 217, which housed a single 13mm machine gun.

Early in the war, however, it became clear that nothing short of turrets with fully powered traverse and elevation would provide adequate protection from fighter attack. Such systems had to be able to slew the guns rapidly at rates of the order of 50 degrees per second, then be fine enough to swing or elevate the guns at minimum speeds of the order of $\frac{1}{4}$ degree per second. This was achieved and it was a favourite trick of RAF gunners to stick a pencil in one of the gun barrels and sign their names on a card held in front of the weapon, to

The simplest form of powered turret employed power for coarse traverse, leaving the gunner to make manual fine corrections in traverse and in elevation. The turret of this type depicted is the DL 131 fitted to the Dornier 217E, carrying a 13 mm Rheinmetall-Borsig MG 131. *Redemann*

demonstrate the ease with which the system could be controlled. With such powered systems there was no fundamental limit to the number of guns that could be fitted to a turret, though for practical reasons there were never more than four.

Early in the war only one bomber type, the LeO 451, carried anything more powerful than rifle-calibre machine guns for its defence. For daylight operations in the face of fighter defences heavier weapons were necessary, however. The .5-in (12.7mm) calibre machine gun gave the best compromise between weight and hitting power and as the war progressed it became the most used weapon for bomber defence.

Typical of the powered turrets of the mid-war period was the American Sperry mid-upper turret fitted to the B-17. Electro-hydraulically powered, it weighed just under 1,000 pounds complete with two .5-in machine guns each with 400 rounds, and protective armour for the gunner; the guns were electrically fired and there was an electrical system to feed the ammunition to the guns. The guns could be traversed through the full 360 degrees at rates of up to 45 degrees per second, and elevated from the horizontal to 85 degrees at rates of up to 30 degrees per second.

The provision of defence for the underside of bombers raised severe problems. Early in the war several bomber types carried retractable 'dustbin' ventral turrets for this purpose; but if they were lowered, the drag of these poorly streamlined cylinders clipped 20 to 30 mph off the bomber's speed just when it least wanted to slow down. These turrets saw little operational use and were soon removed from those aircraft which had been fitted with them. The only really successful manned underneath-turret was the American Sperry ball type, fitted to the B-17 and the B-24. Electro-hydraulically powered, this turret was unique in that it housed the gunner lying on his back; it had therefore to be one of the largest and heaviest turrets to go into service, with a diameter of 44 inches and a weight of 1,290 pounds including the two .5-in guns, ammunition and armour.

The manned power-operated gun turret was

to see most air forces through the war. But by
1942 technology had something rather better to
offer: the remotely controlled barbette.
Compared with the manned turret, the
remotely controlled barbette conferred eight
major advantages. First, there was a better view
for the gunner; since the sighting station was
divorced from the gun mounting, the gunner
could be placed where he could get the best
possible view of incoming fighters. Secondly
there were the improved fields of fire; the guns
could be placed where they had the best
possible fields of fire, regardless of whether this
position was accessible or convenient for the
gunner (this was particularly useful for
underneath defence). Thirdly, there was
improved weight distribution; by separating
the man from his guns, the latter could be
positioned in the tail with less movement of the
aircraft's centre of gravity. Fourthly, there was

The 'dustbin' gun position of the Whitley
bomber, mounting two .303-in machine guns,
shown in the retracted and extended positions.
Although such turrets were fitted to several
bomber types in service at the beginning of the
war, when they were lowered they slowed the
bomber to such an extent that their use in action
was limited and they were soon removed from all
aircraft. *Crown Copyright*

The fully-powered Sperry mid-upper turret fitted
to the B-17 Fortress; the weapons were .5-in
Brownings. *USAF*

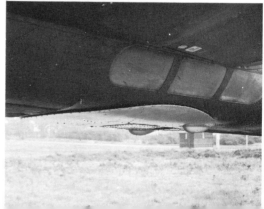

reduced drag; the sighting station and the barbette could be made smaller and streamlined better, so that their combined drag was far less than that from a manned turret. Fifthly, there was less to rotate with the guns; the later manned turrets, with their heavier guns and the necessary ammunition feed and cartridge ejection systems, left little room for the gunner within the space constraints of a rotatable turret. Sixthly, reduced effect from flash; since the gunner was remote from his weapons he was less likely to be blinded by their muzzle flash during an engagement (this was particularly important at night). Seventhly, ease of pressurization; it was far easier to pressurize a static sighting station than a movable manned turret. Eighthly, there was the offer of concentrated fire power; with remote control it was technically possible for a gunner to control more than one barbette, and thus bring concentrated fire to bear on an approaching fighter.

The first remotely controlled armament system to see operational use was that fitted to the German Messerschmitt 210 fighter-bomber, which entered service in the summer of 1942. This aircraft had an FDL 131 barbette on either side of the fuselage, each with a single 13mm MG 131 machine gun. Without ammunition the complete system weighed about 450 pounds and between them the two barbettes provided a field of fire far better than

The bomber type with the most powerful defensive armament of the mid-war period was the Russian Pe-8. The dorsal and rear turrets each carried a 20 mm ShVAK fast-firing cannon, while in the unusual open positions at the rear of the inboard engine nacelles there was a single hand-held 12.7 mm UBS machine gun.

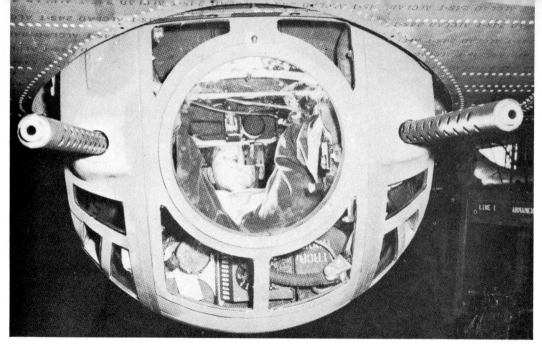

The only really successful manned underneath gun position was the Sperry ball turret fitted to the American B-17 and B-24 bombers; the gunner lay on his back, sighting the guns through his open legs. *Boeing*

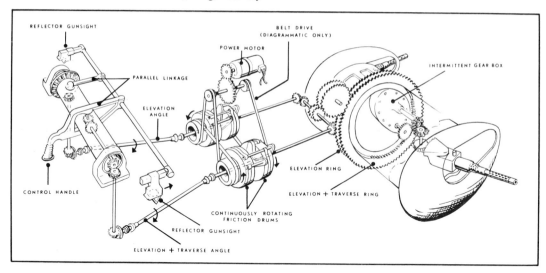

Schematic diagram showing the method of operation of the FDL 131 remotely controlled gun system. The first such system to be used in action, it was fitted to the German Messerschmitt 210 and 410 fighter-bombers. The aircraft's wireless operator aimed the guns, using one of the reflector sights fitted on either side of his position. By moving the sight on the target with the control handle, the gunner 'clutched-in' the out-going drive shaft to one or both of the continuously-rotating friction drums and thus traversed and elevated one of the guns until it was aligned with the target. The guns were able to traverse between 45 degrees outboard and 2 degrees inboard, and elevate or depress to 70 degrees, of the fuselage centre line.

would have been possible for a single manned turret. For the gunner's peace of mind, the guns were fitted with a simple interrupter system which prevented him from shooting bits off the aircraft if they got in the way. In the event the Me 210 was a flop, but that had nothing to do with the remotely controlled armament. The same system was fitted to the more successful Me 410, where it also functioned satisfactorily.

Several bomber types of the late-war period were fitted with remotely controlled gun barbettes, but by far the most impressive

A Messerschmitt 410 fighter-bomber, showing the FDL 131 remotely controlled gun barbette with its 13-mm Rheinmetall-Borsig MG 131.

The remotely controlled rear-upper barbette of a B-29 with two .5-in machine guns; the rear-upper and starboard waist sighting positions can also be seen. *Boeing*

The most powerful defensive gun position fitted to any bomber during the Second World War was that at the rear of some models of the B-29, which went into action carrying a 20 mm M-2 cannon and two .5-in Browning machine guns on a common power-driven mounting. *Boeing*

defensive system to see service was that manufactured by GEC for the American B-29 Superfortress. As used during the war this employed five gun mountings: above the forward fuselage (with four .5-in guns); above the rear fuselage (two .5-in guns); below the forward fuselage (two .5-in guns); below the rear fuselage (two .5-in guns); and in the tail (two .5-in guns and a 20mm cannon). To control these there were five sighting stations:

Diagram showing the permutations of gun barbettes and sighting positions that were possible with the GEC defensive armament system fitted to the B-29. All barbettes were fitted with electrical interrupter gear, to prevent their firing while they were pointing at any part of the aircraft. The tail gunner (1) had control of his own guns (A) only. The waist gunners (2) had primary control of the aft lower barbette (B) and secondary control of the lower forward barbette (D) and the tail guns (A). The rear-upper gunner (3) co-ordinated the fire of all of the other gunners and had sole control of the rear-upper barbette (C) and secondary control of the forward-upper barbette (E). The bombardier in the nose (4) had primary control of the two forward barbettes (D and E). Having taken control of more than one barbette, a gunner could use them simultaneously to engage an attacking fighter.

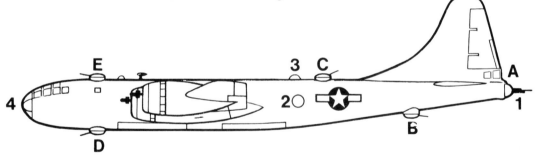

in the extreme nose, above the rear fuselage, on either side of the rear fuselage and in the tail. A clever hand-over system enabled the control of the various barbettes to be put in the hands of the men best able to use them, while a computer corrected for the angular difference between the sighting station and the guns. This system marked the zenith in defensive armament design during the Second World War.

On the subject of defensive armament, mention should be made of the technically interesting (if tactically useless) fixed *rearwards firing* weapons fitted to some German aircraft. Some Dornier 217s, for example, carried two or four 7.9mm machine guns on a fixed mounting in the rear fuselage. Sighting was by means of a periscopic sight fitted in the roof of the pilot's position. The sighting image seen by the pilot was upside-down and back-to-front, so that a fighter closing from above and to starboard looked in the sight as though it were below and to port. This false presentation aided sighting, however, because the pilot had only to fly his aircraft as though the fighter was in front, to bring his guns to bear. The system fell down because if he were to hit the fighter, the bomber pilot had to fly his aircraft so as to give his attacker a perfect zero-deflection shot. Since fighters invariably carried an armament far heavier than that fixed in the rear of the Do

A Dornier 217E fitted with a pair of fixed rearwards-firing 7.9 mm Mauser MG 81 machine guns; the barrels are just visible protruding from the extreme end of the tail cone. Aiming was by means of the rearwards-looking periscopic sight protruding above the pilot's position. Although of technical interest, the fixed rearwards-firing gun was tactically almost useless. Powered by two 1,600 horse power BMW 801 radials, the bomber had a maximum speed of 320 mph; carrying 2,000 pounds of bombs, it had an effective operational radius of about 450 miles. *Redemann*

217, it was hardly surprising that the German crews preferred to take evasive action when they were attacked and thus forgo the dubious protection afforded by their fixed rearwards-firing guns.

The evolution of aircraft gunsights is covered in some detail in *World War II Fighter Conflict* and it is not intended to repeat the description here. Suffice it to say that bombers began the war with simple ring-and-bead sights and progressed to reflector sights; at the close of the conflict many British and American bombers carried gyroscopically predicting sights which greatly increased the accuracy of their fire.

For the defence of night bombers, the main problem was one of detecting the enemy fighter before it reached a firing position. And, once it had been detected, violent evasive action was usually far more effective than return fire. During the mid-war period British and German night bombers were fitted with simple rearwards looking radars, code-named 'Monica' and *Neptun* respectively, to provide warning of fighters approaching from behind. Both devices proved disappointing in service. By that stage of the war the bombers were attacking in concentrated streams, which meant that there were usually several aircraft on the radar throughout the course of the mission; in other words, the sets cried 'Wolf!' so many times when none was present, that their indications came to be ignored. Even worse, the Luftwaffe developed a rather clever direction-finder code-named *Flensburg* which enabled its night fighters to home on the emissions from 'Monica'; when the RAF got to hear about it, the tail warning sets were stripped out of virtually all bombers.

Potentially more effective for the defence of night bombers was the airborne gunlaying radar, developed in Britain under the code-name 'Village Inn'. This comprised a rather advanced radar set, small enough to be fitted to the rear turret of a heavy bomber. The scanner dish was linked to the guns and traversed and elevated with them. The radar picture was

'Village Inn' gunlaying radar fitted to the rear turret of a Halifax bomber; the guns were .5-in Brownings.

projected on to the gunner's sight complete with ranging information. Now it was technically possible to engage enemy fighters at night beyond visual range. The problem of identification remained, however: if gunners were allowed to open up at anything behind them, the system could well destroy many more bombers than it saved. When 'Village Inn' entered service in the summer of 1944, gunners were permitted to engage only those targets that could be positively identified as hostile. A special nose-mounted infra-red identification system was produced and installed in many bombers, but the war ended before all could be fitted and gunners be permitted to use 'Village Inn' to its full effect.

Slowing the Defences

During the first three years of the war there was a massive influx of electronic equipment into the air defence systems of all the major powers: radar for early warning, for the ground control of fighters, to direct anti-aircraft guns and searchlights and to assist night fighters to locate their prey; also important were the radio channels which linked the fighters with their ground controllers. An air defence system could be likened to a chain, a chain which performed effectively only if each of the links functioned properly.

As air defences became more dependent upon radar and radio systems for efficient operation, consideration was given to the jamming of these. If one or more links in the defensive chain could be weakened, even for a short time, the defence's reactions would be slowed; if they were slowed enough, the losses suffered during the bombers' passage through a defended area would be greatly reduced.

The first serious attempt to provide jamming support for bombers occurred at the end of 1942, when RAF bombers began carrying 'Mandrel' transmitters. 'Mandrel' radiated noise on the frequency used by the German *Freya* early warning radar, and was effective in reducing the range at which the radar could plot targets. The Germans replied by bringing out new versions of *Freya* which worked on different frequencies, to avoid the jamming; so began the battle in the ether, that was to grow in intensity as the war progressed.

Soon after the introduction of 'Mandrel', RAF bombers also began to carry a simple modification to their radio sets code-named 'Tinsel': a microphone installed in one of the engine nacelles and wired into the aircraft's wireless transmitter. The bomber's radio operator used his receiver to search the frequency band used by the German fighter controllers; when he found one of their channels he tuned in his transmitter, switched in the microphone and broadcast the engine noises to blot out the controller's instructions. 'Tinsel' was only moderately effective, because it lacked the high power necessary to jam radio communications. Later a purpose-built communications jammer, code-named 'Jostle', was installed in some RAF aircraft; it radiated a high-powered row on the German fighter

Safe to handle, yet devastating in its effect: the author's young daughter poses with a piece of Window similar to the type which neutralised the German night defences in the summer of 1943.

control channels, a cross between a police siren and the bagpipes, which proved effective enough.

As well as transmitted jamming, there was a simpler method that could be used to jam radar: the release of lengths of aluminium foil, cut to roughly one half the wavelength of the radar they were intended to counter. Released in small bundles, the foil gave the appearance of numerous false targets on the radar; released in massive quantities, it could blot out the radar screens altogether. During the final two years of the war this form of countermeasure saw large-scale use, known as 'Window' in the RAF, 'Chaff' or 'Rope' in the US Army Air Force and the US Navy, *Dueppel* in the Luftwaffe and *Giman-shi* in the Japanese Army and Navy. By the final stage of the war the rate of consumption of the foil, in the USAAF alone, was running at about 2,000 tons per month.

The value of jamming in saving bombers from destruction is impossible to assess accurately: one cannot say with certainty which bombers would have been shot down and which would have survived, had there been no jamming. There is, however, good reason to believe that jamming saved the Royal Air Force something of the order of one thousand night bombers and their crews, between the beginning of 1943 and the end of the war in Europe; in this context it is relevant to mention that it was not until the final year of the war that the operational strength of RAF Bomber Command actually reached one thousand aircraft. In the case of the other great user of jamming, the US Army Air Force, the great majority of its bombing attacks were made by day when the enemy fighters could intercept and the AA gunners could aim their weapons visually. As a result, the jamming did not have so great an effect as it did at night; nevertheless, it is reasonable to say that something of the order of four hundred American bombers were saved by the use of radar countermeasures.

Only on two occasions did radar countermeasures bring about the collapse of an air defence system. The first was during the series of attacks on Hamburg in July 1943, when 'Window' was introduced and achieved considerable effect due to its surprise; the breakdown was only temporary, however, and the German defences recovered rapidly. The second occasion was in 1945, when during the night attacks the Americans neutralised the primitive Japanese radar systems by transmitting jamming and releasing metal foil on a large scale. For the rest of the war the effect of the jamming was a continual, if less spectacular, reduction in losses by something of the order of one-sixth.

Finding the Target

For bomber crews flying over land by day through clear skies, navigation using ground features was a relatively simple matter. But if they had to fly over long stretches of sea, or above cloud, or at night, accurate navigation was considerably more difficult. Unless ground features were visible, even a good bomber crew could drift far off the intended track without their being aware of it. Hence the need for electronic aids to assist crews to find their targets.

The 1930s had seen a rapid development in radio navigational techniques, spurred by airlines trying to maintain schedules through changeable weather. The first aids fitted to aircraft were simple radio direction finders, to enable airliners to home from city to city using broadcast transmitters or radio beacons. The next stage was to set up directional beacons on the ground which radiated beams down set routes, thus establishing a sort of 'highway' through the sky. A clever variation of this was the German Lorenz system, a short range

The Lorenz Beam.

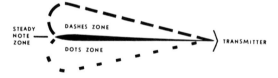

ground transmitter which radiated a double beam with morse dots on one side and morse dashes on the other; the beams overlapped and the dots and dashes interlocked, so that there was a narrow lane down which a steady-note signal was radiated. During the late 1930s Lorenz transmitters were installed at numerous airfields, to assist aircraft to approach and land in conditions of poor visibility.

Meanwhile, the Luftwaffe began experimenting with Lorenz beams to guide bombers to their targets. The system which resulted, code-named *Knickebein*, amounted to a super high power Lorenz ground transmitter, with a huge oblong aerial array 315 feet wide and 100 feet high. This huge array squeezed the dot and dash radiations into narrow beams, with a steady-note lane only a third of a degree wide; this meant that the lane was only one mile wide at a distance of 180 miles from the transmitter, a remarkable achievement for the time. The aerial was pivoted at the centre and mounted on bogies which ran on rails, so that the beam could be aligned on a target with great accuracy. By arranging for a beam from a second *Knickebein* transmitter to cross that from the first at the bomb release point, a bomber crew could be told precisely when to release and they could achieve reasonable accuracy even though it was dark or the target was hidden by cloud. It was all clever stuff, particularly as the beam signals could be picked up using the Lorenz airfield approach receivers which were a standard fitting to all Luftwaffe bombers.

Many people would have rested on their laurels, having perfected a system like *Knickebein* which was so far in advance of anything similar to guide bombers. But the Luftwaffe pushed the use of Lorenz-type beams a stage further with the so-called *X-Geraet* precision bombing system. To fine down the steady-note lane still further, *X-Geraet* operated on a wavelength somewhat shorter than that of *Knickebein*. It employed not two beams but four: an approach beam and three cross beams which intersected it at set positions in front of the target. The pilot simply held the aircraft in the centre of the approach beam and

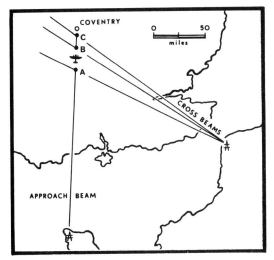

The layout of the X-beams during the attack on Coventry on November 14th 1940.

A The first cross beam served as a warning that the aircraft was nearing the target and that it had to get into the centre of the approach beam.

B As he heard the steady-note signal from the second beam, 20 kilometres from the bomb-release point, the observer pressed a button to start the bombing clock.

C As he heard the steady-note signal from the third beam, 5 kilometres from the aiming point, the observer again pressed the button on his bombing clock. The moving hand of the clock stopped, and a second hand moved at three times its speed to catch it up. When the two hands overlapped a pair of electrical contacts closed and the bombs were released automatically.

the observer operated a special clock when he heard the steady-note lane signals from the second and third cross beams; this primed the system, which *automatically* released the bombs as the aircraft passed the release point. Technically this was a pretty sophisticated system, and it was working before the war began. The combination of the clock and the beams provided accurate data on the bomber's speed over the ground, one of the most important things required for precision bombing once the aircraft was routed accurately over the target. *X-Geraet* was considerably more accurate than *Knickebein*, but it was also a lot more complex. To use it aircraft had to carry special receivers, and to get

the most out of it the crews required special training. Late in 1939 the world's first precision night attack unit, *Kampfgruppe 100*, became operational flying Heinkel 111s fitted with the *X-Geraet*.

When the air war began in earnest late in the spring of 1940, the brilliantly-conceived German beam systems were used in a manner that was tactically naïve. *Knickebein* was tested out over Britain during some small-scale probing attacks and its secret was soon revealed. Deeply impressed by the cleverness of the enemy system and shocked by its possible implications, the Royal Air Force hastily put together a jamming organisation to counter it. The result was that when the Luftwaffe really needed *Knickebein*, to guide bombers during the large-scale night attacks in September 1940, the jamming was just about powerful enough to render the system unusable over much of Britain (though the deliberate bending of the beams, which has been alleged in several accounts, never actually happened).

That still left the *X-Geraet*. *Kampfgruppe 100* was used as a pathfinder unit, to start fires at the target which the rest of the bomber force could attack. These tactics were used during the devastating attack on Coventry in mid-November 1940. Within a short time, however, the RAF head learned the secrets of the *X-Geraet* and it too was neutralized with jamming.

Early in 1941 the Luftwaffe began using a third beam system, the *Y-Geraet*, which employed only a single ground station. The bomber approached its target flying up a rather complicated beam quite different from that used by the other systems. To measure the distance *along* the beam, the ground station radiated a separate ranging signal which the aircraft picked up and re-radiated. Operators at the ground station were then able to compute the position of the aircraft with great accuracy and, when it reached the bomb release point, they radioed orders to the crew to release the bombs. Alas, in the face of jamming, the *Y-Geraet* performed no better than its predecessors. The British jamming organisation had great sport injecting its own false ranging signals into the system, with the result that the German ground operators obtained all sorts of odd range measurements which bore no relation to the position of the bombers they were supposed to be controlling.

It is easy to make light of the German beam systems and their inability to perform effectively in the face of jamming. Nevertheless, before the jamming became fully effective each of them proved of value in guiding bombers to targets at night; and afterwards they were useful in assisting navigation along part of the route. The significance of the German systems falls into relief only if we consider how Bomber Command of the RAF got on without any such aids during the first two and a half years of its operations against Germany. If in general the German night bombing against Britain was mediocre, that of the RAF was miserable. An inquiry in mid-1941 based on photographic evidence revealed that only *one in three* of the RAF bomber crews had placed their bombs within *five miles* of the aiming point; for the Ruhr area, with its almost permanent blanket of industrial haze, only *one in ten* had done so.

As Mr Churchill chided Sir Charles Portal, his Chief of Air Staff: 'It is an awful thought that perhaps three quarters of our bombs go astray... If we could make it half and half we should virtually have doubled our bombing power.'

The shameful revelations provided a mighty impetus to the development of electronic navigational systems in Britain. The first to go into service, early in 1942, was GEE. This system employed three ground transmitters working in concert, to radiate a complex train of pulses in a pre-determined order. Using a special receiver, the aircraft navigator could measure the differences in the time of arrival of the various pulses; he then read off his position from a special map. Because the distances from the transmitters were much greater, GEE was not so accurate over Germany as *Knickebein* had been over Britain. Nevertheless there was a marked improvement in bombing accuracy —

Silent but deadly: an Oboe ground transmitting station, showing the two sets of aerials to enable two aircraft to be controlled simultaneously during their bombing runs. *Crown Copyright*

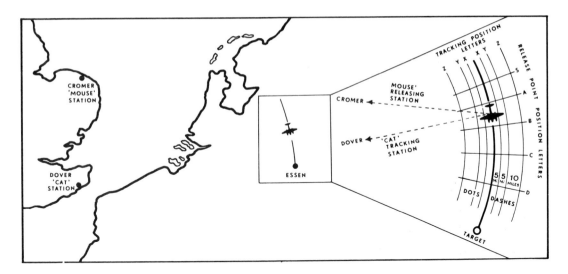

until the Germans showed that they too could play the jamming game.

Early in 1943 the RAF introduced its first radar precision bombing system, 'Oboe'. This device exploited the fact that a radar can measure the range of an aircraft with considerable accuracy (though in measuring bearing it is somewhat less accurate). The system employed two ground stations. One tracked the aircraft as it flew along an arc of constant range running through the target, and passed correction signals if the aircraft deviated from this arc. Meanwhile the second station measured the range also and, when the aircraft was observed to be at the previously-computed bomb release point, the order was given to release.

To extend the range of 'Oboe' to that limited by the curvature of the earth, the aircraft carried a pair of repeater transmitters which amplified the signals before returning them to the ground stations; the repeater sets were small and light and could easily be fitted into existing aircraft. Under operational conditions 'Oboe' proved extremely accurate. Its main disadvantage was that its use was limited to the area within about 280 miles of each of the ground transmitters which had, of course, to be located in friendly territory; a further problem was that a pair of ground transmitter-receivers could control only one bomber at a time during its bombing run, which might last up to ten

The method of operation of Oboe: one ground station (the 'Cat') tracked the aircraft along an arc of constant radius passing through the target; a second ground station (the 'Mouse') carried out continual range measurements on the target and indicated by radio when the aircraft was at the bomb release point.

minutes. In fact an arc 280 miles from the east coast of Britain took in all of the important Ruhr industrial area in Germany. 'Oboe' was fitted to Mosquito pathfinder aircraft, which marked the targets for the main force of bombers. The Germans found it difficult to jam, especially in its later short-wavelength versions.

There can be no doubt that the Germans were mightily impressed by 'Oboe', for they copied the principle for their *Egon* system which was used during the attacks on Britain early in 1944.

The British GEE-H and the American 'Shoran' systems were essentially similar to 'Oboe' but their transmissions were initiated from, and the computations were made in, the aircraft. The ground stations had only to repeat back pulses, which meant that they could be used simultaneously by hundreds of aircraft without the system becoming saturated.

All of the electronic aids described so far suffered from the basic disadvantage that their use was limited to the area within about 280 miles of the ground transmitters.

If the bombers were to attack accurately at

greater distances, a system was required that was independent of the ground stations. Early in 1943 such a system went into service with the RAF pathfinder units: the H2S radar. H2S was, for its time, an extremely advanced type of radar which scanned the ground beneath the aircraft. The returning echoes came strongest from built-up areas, less strongly from open countryside and least strongly from water areas. By displaying the echo signals on a cathode-ray tube it was, therefore, possible to produce a fairly good representation of the surrounding terrain which could be compared with a map of the area. In its initial versions the size and weight of the H2S installation limited its application to heavy bombers. Effectively the device had no maximum range: it could be used out to the maximum range of the aircraft carrying it. Bombing accuracy depended on the nature of the terrain round the target: some targets, for example Hamburg situated on a wide river estuary, produced very distinctive echoes on H2S; other targets, especially those

A Consolidated B-24 Liberator, its H2X radome extended, seen releasing high explosive and incendiary bombs at the target. *USAF*

inland surrounded by broken terrain, produced less distinct echoes and were more difficult to find.

H2S in its Mark I, II and III versions served the RAF until the end of the war. A few were also delivered to the US Army Air Force where they were fitted into B-17s and B-24s, until that service's similar H2X system was ready. The only things that could be said against this device was that it was large and heavy, and its signals could be intercepted by the enemy fairly easily. The Germans built up a ground organisation to track the movements of bombers by their H2S and H2X emissions and even introduced a special receiver, code-named *Naxos*, to enable night fighters to home on their radiations. Since the Second World War some form of ground-scanning radar has been a standard fitting to all medium and heavy bomber types.

An H2S indicator, fitted in the navigator's position of a Lancaster. *Secker, via Garbett/Goulding*

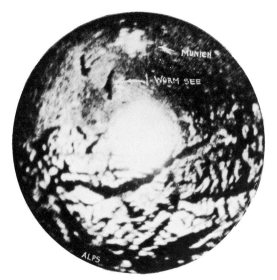

An H2X picture, taken over the south of Germany. As is always the case for such radar-scope pictures, the camera shutter was left open for one complete sweep of the rotating timebase; as a result, the timebase itself is not visible. The city of Munich, at the top of the picture, and the Alps extending across the lower half of the picture, throw back strong returns. The Ammersee and the Wuermsee, two lakes to the south west and south of Munich respectively, throw back hardly any echoes and appear as dark patches on the radar screen. *USAF*

Sighting the Bombs

In the end, the destructiveness of an attack depended on the accuracy with which the bombs were placed. Although beam and radar aiming systems did play a progressively more important part, especially for pathfinder operations, the vast majority of bombs were aimed visually. Moreover, although there were some spectacular exceptions, by far the greater part of all attacks were launched by bombers flying horizontally at high altitude. We shall, therefore, now examine the types of sights employed for high-level horizontal bombing; there were two basic types, the vector sight and the tachometric sight.

With the vector sight the bomb aimer had to set in the aircraft's speed and altitude, the bomb ballistic data and the estimated wind speed and direction. He was then presented with a sighting cross (formed either of pieces of wire or lines of light on a reflecting screen), which indicated the point on the ground the bombs would strike if they were released at that instant. The sighting cross was extended up the line of approach and the bomb aimer directed the pilot to fly the aircraft so that this extended line passed through the target; when the sighting cross coincided with the target, he released the bombs.

The simple vector sight worked well enough in aircraft of the Hinaidi era, which could make flat (ie unbanked) turns during bombing runs with little difficulty. With monoplane bombers

The British Mark XIV was the most advanced type of vector bombsight to see service during the war. The sighting graticule was projected on to the stabilized glass at the front of the sight. *Crown Copyright*

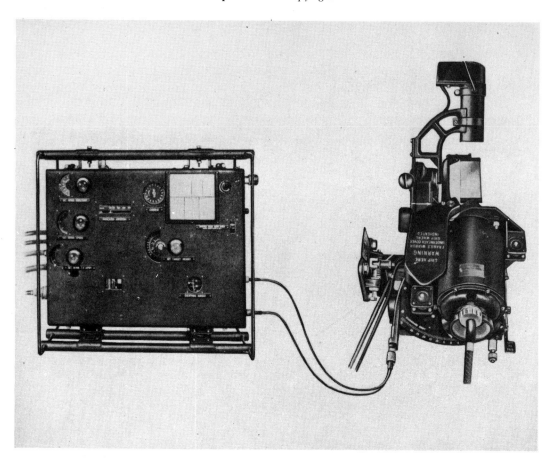

it was a different matter, however; with these aerodynamically cleaner aircraft flat turns could be made only slowly, or the bomber would slide sideways through the air. As a result the vector sights in use at the beginning of the war, the British Mark IX, the French Bronzavia and the Italian Jozza, gave only mediocre results. It was this lack of accuracy that had persuaded the Germans to concentrate on aircraft able to dive-bomb, a mode of attack that gave far better results but which introduced a quite different set of problems.

The RAF saw that the vector principle was the best for its requirements, for reasons that will become clear shortly, and pressed ahead with the development of a gyro-stabilised vector sight. The result was the famous Mark XIV, which entered service late in 1942 and continued in use with small modifications long after the war. This sight gave good results and allowed banked turns to be made during the bombing run. An interesting feature was the so-called 'bomber's mate', an elaborate analogue computer which correlated the various factors associated with aiming.

The tachometric sight was fundamentally different from the vector sight. With the former, the bomb aimer viewed the target through a sighting telescope during the bombing run. The telescope was moved by a variable-speed electric motor and, having set into the sight the aircraft's altitude and the bombs' ballistic data, the bomb aimer operated controls to hold the telescope's sighting graticule over the target. The platform supporting the telescope was gyro-stabilized and the act of holding the telescope on the target fed precise information on the aircraft's movement over the ground into the sighting computer. The computer generated course correction signals, which could be presented on

The American Norden and the German Lotfe 7D (right) tachometric bombsights. The tachometric sight gave more accurate results than the vector sight if there were clear skies and there was no smoke obscuring the target during a long bombing run; if conditions were not ideal, however, it was the vector sight that gave the better results.

a directional indicator in front of the pilot. As the aircraft neared the target, the angle of the telescope approached the vertical; when it reached the release angle calculated by the sight's computer, a pair of electrical contacts closed and the bombs were released automatically. Representative sights employing the tachometric principle were the German Lotfe (which gave results comparable with those from diving attacks and led to the dropping of this requirement), the American Norden and the British SABS. Although each nation made grandiose claims for its own type of sight, technically they were closely comparable; differences in performance depended on operator skills rather than on the superiority of one type of tachometric sight over another.

Tachometric sights generated electrical correction signals, and in the later versions of the Norden and Lotfe sights these could be fed directly into the aircraft's automatic pilot. As a result, the bomb aimer was provided with the facility to 'fly' the aircraft to the bomb release point by holding his sighting telescope over the target.

Under ideal conditions the tachometric sight was rather more accurate than the stabilized vector type of sight. Typical operational 50 per cent circular errors* for attacks from 10,000 feet were about 100 yards for tachometric and about 225 yards for stabilized vector sights, in each case considering daylight attacks in clear skies; as altitude increased, so did the errors. Tactically, however, ideal conditions with clear skies up to 20,000 feet often did not exist. To hold the sighting telescope on the target for long enough for the tachometric sight to compute the release point, an undeviating

*The 50 per cent circular error is the radius of a circle, centred on the target, into which the best 50 per cent of a number of individually-aimed bombs or sticks of bombs will fall, when released using a given method of sighting or aiming. Errors could be greatly increased if the bomb aimers were not fully trained, if the visibility was poor, or if the defences were reacting powerfully. The errors mentioned here are, therefore, intended to give only an approximate idea of the comparative accuracy of the various bomb sights and aiming methods.

bombing run of at least 20 seconds was necessary; at night, if the target could not be seen from far enough away, or if there was smoke or cloud concealing the target for part of the run, the vector sight gave the better results. The latter indicated the bombs' point of impact at any instant during the bombing run, allowing the aimer to exploit a fleeting glimpse of the target; for this reason, the stabilized vector was the more practicable type of sight for general operational use.

Smoke from fires started at the target by bombers in the initial waves frequently concealed the aiming point from those in following waves, with the result that bombing accuracy gradually deteriorated during the course of the attack.

A subtle answer to this problem, possible only with vector type sights, was to use an offset aiming point. A distinctive aiming point close to the target was chosen prior to the attack, and marked by pathfinder aircraft. During their approach the crews of other pathfinder aircraft had measured the wind in the target area and passed their findings to the Master Bomber. In the Master Bomber a specially picked navigator averaged out these winds; the result was then combined vectorially with the distance between the marker at the offset aiming point and the actual target. In this way the navigator worked out a 'false wind' setting, which was then broadcast to the rest of the incoming bombers and set into the bomb sights. The bomb aimers sighted on the marker at the offset aiming point and, because of the false wind setting in their sights, the bombs hit the target. Since the offset aiming point was some distance from the target, smoke from fires at the latter did not conceal it.

A slightly less accurate variation of this technique, possible with both tachometric and vector sights, was for crews to run in from a set direction to an offset aiming point as though they were to bomb it, then fly on for a predetermined number of seconds before releasing the bombs. This type of attack, known as the 'Timed Overshoot', was frequently used by both day and night bombers during the closing stages of the war.

For most of the war the general accuracy of night bombing was considerably worse than that achieved by day, with 50 per cent circular errors often more than ten times as great. By the final part of the war, however, Royal Air Force night bombing techniques had evolved to the point where well-trained and practised crews bombing on offset markers, planted accurately by pathfinder Mosquitoes flying at low altitude, were able to achieve results comparable with those by day.

2. Six of the Best

*The race is not always to the swiftest nor the
  fight to the strongest.
But that's the way you bet.*

attributed to SAMUEL GOLDWYN

   *In this chapter we shall examine in detail six
of the most important bomber types which saw
service during the Second World War: the
German Heinkel 111 and Junkers 88; the
British Lancaster and Mosquito; and the
American B-24 Liberator and B-25 Mitchell.
Given below are excerpts from reports on the
operational trials with these aircraft, carried
out by the Air Fighting Development Unit of
the Royal Air Force.*

The Heinkel 111H

   *The Heinkel 111 first entered service in 1937
and by the beginning of the war the H and P
versions of this aircraft equipped the units
forming the backbone of the German bomber
force. The He 111 held this position for the first
year of the war, after which it was gradually
replaced in many units by the Junkers 88. The
tests described took place in September 1941
and the remarks in the report are relevant to
that time.*

Brief Description of the Aircraft

   The Heinkel 111H is a low-wing twin-
engined monoplane fitted with Jumo 211
engines of 1,200 horse power each. It is capable
of carrying a bomb load of 4,400 pounds.

Crew

   The crew usually consists of five by day and
four by night: pilot; observer, who combines
the duties of navigator, bomb aimer and front
gunner; an upper gunner who is the wireless
operator; a lower gunner; and a third gunner
who mans the beam guns by day.

Pilot's Cockpit

   The pilot's cockpit is situated over the
leading edge of the mainplane. The aircraft is
normally flown with the pilot enclosed, but he
can raise his seat together with the controls so
that his head projects through a sliding hatch in
the roof of the cockpit. This position is used for
taxying, take-off and landing, and gives a very

The layout of the Heinkel 111H.

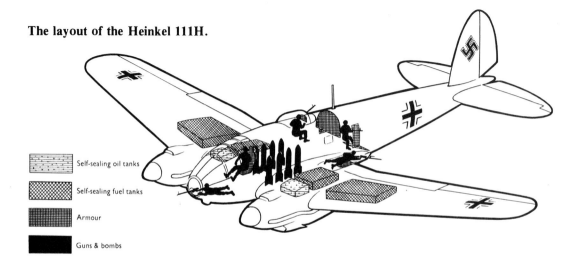

Self-sealing oil tanks

Self-sealing fuel tanks

Armour

Guns & bombs

Close-up of the nose of the He 111H, showing the excellent visibility forwards and downwards enjoyed by the observer. Powered by two 1,200 horse power Jumo 211 in-line engines, the bomber had a maximum speed of 258 mph; carrying 2,000 pounds of bombs, it had an effective operational radius of about 500 miles. *Jope*

Inside the He 111, showing the poor visibility for the pilot in the enclosed cockpit. For landing the pilot had to raise his seat so that his head projected through a sliding hatch in the roof of the cockpit. *von Lossberg*

good all-round view. The enclosed position which is normally used for operational flying, allows only a limited view. Upwards and ahead from this position the view is restricted by the main instrument panel, and to the starboard beam it is poor, owing to the engine and massive window frames of the cockpit. The pilot is blind on the starboard quarter, and to the rear, but on the port side his view is moderately good.

Navigator/Front Gunner

The control column can be swung over opposite the navigator's seat so that he can act as second pilot, but there are no other flying controls within his reach. When lying forward over the bomb sight or manning the front gun his view is good, as the pointed nose is almost entirely constructed of perspex.

Upper Gunner/Wireless Operator

The upper gunner sits in the dorsal position which is just forward of the trailing edge of the mainplane and has a good all-round view. His seat consists of a piece of canvas slung across the fuselage and attached at each end to the bottom of the Scarff ring for the gun. His feet are supported on an iron ring. His weight roughly compensates for that of the gun and enables him to rotate the Scarff ring freely. His head and shoulders are protected from the slipstream by a sliding cupola, but if he wishes to move his gun more than 20 degrees from the tail, he has to push the cupola right back which makes his position extremely cold and draughty. It is presumed that he accepts the restricted arc of fire at night, as the cold would otherwise be unbearable, and pushes back the hood after the action has begun. The wireless equipment is on the port side of the aircraft and the altimeter and blind landing indicator are fitted in convenient positions.

Lower Gunner

The lower gunner lies in a gondola slung beneath the rear compartment of the fuselage. He is not cramped but the position would be extremely uncomfortable for any lengthy period and he would probably sit on the ledge beneath the beam windows, except when in danger areas. His view downwards and to the side is restricted by sections of armour plate which almost fill the perspex panels, but his view to the rear is good except near the tail, which can be seen only with difficulty.

Beam Gunner

The beam gunner has to kneel on the window ledge or stand astride the fuselage, as his only alternative is to stand on the lower gunner, which no doubt he frequently does in moments of excitement. His view is good.

The bomb compartment completely fills the fuselage between the pilot's cabin and the rear compartment, but there is a cat-walk through it for communication. The normal entrance for the crew is through a hatch in the bottom of the gondola.

Armament Characteristics

The armament of this aircraft is out-of-date and cannot be considered representative of that in an aircraft likely to be met today. As the object of the trials is to provide information useful to fighter pilots, the details of armament given below are not those in the aircraft available, but those actually to be expected in an up-to-date aircraft. The fighter's tactics are worked out accordingly.

A Heinkel 111 usually has a total of six 7.9mm machine guns, mounted in the following manner: one MG 15 in a rotatable ring in the nose, one MG 15 on a Scarff ring in the dorsal position, a single MG 15 on each beam firing out of a window, a fixed MG 17 'scare' gun in the tail [few aircraft carried these] and an MG 15 in the lower gondola firing aft. The latter may be replaced by a 20mm Oerlikon in the latest aircraft [in fact this did not become a standard fitting, though some aircraft did carry a 20mm cannon in the nose gun position]. All guns have ring and bead sights.

Functioning and Handling

These guns were not fired, but from previous tests carried out with an MG 15 from a Ju 88 this type is thought to be a satisfactory and effective weapon. The rate of fire is 1,000 rounds per minute and although the magazines

hold only 75 rounds, they can be changed in 5 seconds. The rate of fire of the 20mm gun is 350 rounds per minute and clips of 15 rounds are used. The MG 15s are in gimbal mountings which give free movement but they compare very unfavourably with the turret mountings used in British aircraft. It is extremely difficult to fire a steady continuous burst and this is confirmed by an analysis of combat reports.

Arcs of Fire

Theoretically every type of fighter attack is covered by at least one gun, but there are certain positions in which the lower gunner has great difficulty in sighting.

Armour

The crew are well protected from astern attacks. The pilot's seat has an armoured back and head-piece. The upper gunner has a face shield and the whole of the upper half of the main cabin directly aft of his position is fitted with a semi-circular cross-section of armour.

Bomb doors open, a He 111H is seen approaching its target. Only 550-pound bombs or smaller weapons could be carried in the internal bomb bay, suspended from their noses and hanging vertically; larger bombs had to be carried externally. *via Schliephake*

The lower half of the cabin is protected by a deflector plate fitted across the bottom of the fuselage behind the entrance hatch. The beam guns have curved shields bolted to the side of the fuselage behind the windows, and the main part of the lower gunner's gondola is protected by slabs of armour except the window through which the gun is mounted. The total weight of armour is 600 pounds. All fuel and oil tanks are self-sealing but there is no protection for the engines.

Tactical Trials

Flying Characteristics

The Heinkel 111 was subject to [flying] restrictions and it was therefore impossible to discover its manoeuvrability [the aircraft had suffered damage when it came down in Britain]. The aircraft was flown light throughout the trials with a crew of four or five, and it gave the impression of having slightly lighter controls than the Wellington. All controls are well harmonised.

The aircraft can be trimmed to fly hands off and instrument flying is particularly easy. No night flying was carried out. Single engine flying was carried out with each airscrew feathered in turn and the aircraft was found perfectly controllable on one engine. It will maintain height easily when unladen at about 140 mph indicated, and can be turned both towards and away from the live engine without difficulty.

Formation Flying. The Heinkel 111 is easy to fly in close formation, being responsive to the throttles and having good deceleration. Flying with the leader on the starboard side is difficult owing to the restricted view, and is possible only on the port side if on the same level as, or below, the leader.

Fighting Manoeuvres

General. The Heinkel 111 was flown in combat with a Spitfire I and a Hurricane II, the fighters using camera guns. The Heinkel appears to fly in a slightly tail-down attitude and this fact should be borne in mind by fighter pilots when making deflection allowances.

Astern Attacks. A fighter attacking from above will be met by the gun in the dorsal position. As this gun is in a gimbal mounting on a Scarff ring, it cannot be manoeuvred very quickly and accurate continuous firing is difficult. The gunner is also liable to hit the Heinkel's rudder, which is sufficiently large to give the fighter some protection. If the fighter attacks from the same level as the Heinkel, or slightly below, he will be shielded from the upper gun by the tailplane but will then be in the line of fire of the fixed MG·17 or of the machine gun or Oerlikon in the gondola. The sights of the lower guns however are frequently obscured by the framework of the gondola and by the rotatable ring on which the gun is mounted. The

Oerlikon can fire about 15 degrees on each side of the tail and will depress to about 20 degrees below the horizontal. As it is extremely difficult to sight it is probable that it will usually be fired directly astern, about 10 degrees down. The fighter's best astern attack therefore is from just above the tail or from about 30 degrees below. He should concentrate on the engines as the fuselage is well armoured. The breakaway should be downwards.

Quarter and Beam Attacks. A quarter or beam attack from above or on the same level can be met by the upper gun and the beam gun. The same difficulties apply to the upper gun as in the astern attack. The beam gun has a fairly good field of fire but accurate shooting will be unlikely owing to the gunner's uncomfortable position. If the attack is delivered from below, the fighter will be met by the beam gun which is unlikely to be accurate and also by the lower gunner who can fire up to 30 degrees on the quarter. The lower gunner finds it difficult to sight as far round as this, and if the aircraft is armed with the Oerlikon cannon he is even more limited. As the Heinkel has no armour protection against quarter attacks, it is clear that this type of attack is the most likely to prove successful and if made from the port side there is a good chance of killing the pilot.

Head-On Attacks. The Heinkel 111 has no protection from head-on attacks and fighters should find this attack effective, particularly against formations relying on mutual support for protection against astern or quarter attacks. The field of fire of the front gun is limited and accurate sighting difficult as the gunner has to move the rotatable window with one hand and fire the gun with the other.

Night Fighter Attacks. Fighters should normally attack from astern and below. If a fine quarter attack on the port side is possible this will reduce the risk of opposition from the cannon. Free gun fighters [ie the Boulton Paul Defiant] should slide in below on the bow, as this area is blind and no return fire is possible.

Slipstream. The slipstream goes up slightly behind the Heinkel 111 and is stronger on the port side. A fighter who keeps well down in an astern attack is unlikely to be worried by it until he is about 100 yards astern.

The Junkers 88A-6

The Junkers 88 was just entering service at the beginning of the war and by mid-1941 it had become the most used German bomber type; it held that position until the virtual collapse of the German bomber arm in the summer of 1944. The A-6 version first appeared early in 1941 and the trial took place the following August.

Brief Description of the Aircraft

The Junkers 88 is a mid-wing twin-engined monoplane, fitted with Jumo 211 engines of 1,200 hp each. It is capable of carrying 6,400 pounds of bombs in which case its range is 550 air miles. Its maximum range is 2,200 miles, but with a bomb load of only 1,100 pounds. It is fitted with dive brakes which permit angles of dive of up to 70 degrees. There is a fully automatic pilot and also provision for a second

control column, which the bomb aimer can use. Other equipment includes de-icing for airscrews and tailplane, and provision for balloon cable cutters in the wings.

Cabin

The crew of four are positioned together in a small compartment well forward. The pilot and the upper gunner, who is also the wireless operator, have comfortable seats and sufficient room to carry out their duties; but conditions for the bomb aimer, and the lower gunner who lies in a gondola slung beneath the starboard side of the cabin, are cramped and uncomfortable. It is not thought possible for the lower gunner to remain at his gun for more than an hour at a time, and he has a small rest seat just above his position. The bomb aimer sits in a cramped position beside the pilot when

The layout of the Junkers 88A-6.

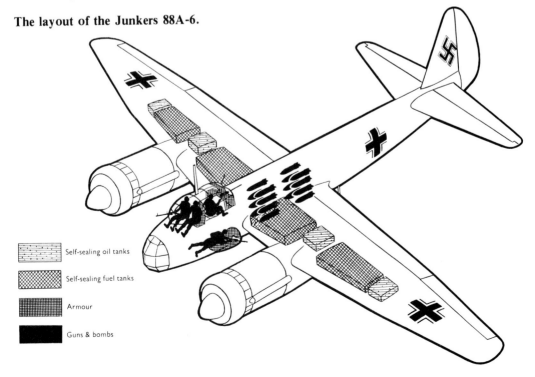

Self-sealing oil tanks

Self-sealing fuel tanks

Armour

Guns & bombs

he is not lying over his sight, which is uncomfortably close to the rudder pedals and bomb switches. The crew cannot exchange positions.

Armament Characteristics

The guns on the aircraft available for trials are four MG 15s in gimbal mountings. Two of these are in the upper rear part of the cabin, set in separate rotatable bullet-proof window rings. The third gun is in the gondola firing aft, and the fourth fires forward mounted on the starboard side of the front of the cabin. The number of rounds available is 1,650 in 22 magazines of 75 rounds each. The magazines are fitted on racks in the side and back of the cabin and in all spaces where there is no other equipment. The armament appears to be the latest and most efficient the Germans have adopted for this aircraft. Earlier models have gimbal mountings only in the rear cockpit cover in place of the rotatable rings and a further similar mounting each side for firing on the beam. These four guns must have seriously obstructed the rear gunner's view and hampered his movements.

Sights

The sights for all guns are 60 mph [deflection] ring and bead. The bead is nearest the gunner's eye and the ring at the muzzle end of the gun.

Functioning

One gun was specially mounted and fired on the ground at stop butts. The three rear guns were fired from the aircraft over the sea. No stoppages occurred and the recoil was negligible at any angle. The rate of fire is 1,000 rounds per minute and there is little smoke or fumes. The ammunition did not appear to be loaded in any definite order, but approximately one round in five was red tracer or green incendiary tracer. The remainder consists of ball, armour-piercing and high explosive. A night firing test was carried out and the tracer did not have a particularly dazzling effect. The general impression is that the gun is very simple and an extremely effective weapon. The time taken to change magazines is 5 seconds.

Area of Fire

The upper rear guns cover a good field of up to about 75 degrees on each beam and 35 degrees in elevation. The lower gun is capable of being fired through an angle of 40 degrees each side from dead astern — but firing to starboard is easier than to port, owing to the position of the gunner with the stock to his right shoulder. The maximum depression of 30 degrees is only obtained astern and is reduced to 15 degrees on each side. There is no blind spot behind the tail. The front gun is very restricted and can be locked if necessary in a horizontal position, presumably so that the pilot can fire it, though in this aircraft there was no method for him to do so.

Armour

The crew are extremely well protected against attacks from the rear and fine quarter. The whole of the back of the cabin is protected by armour and bullet-proof glass as far down as the upper gunner's knees. The lower gunner has a dome of armour plate below him and a semicircular piece of armour which rotates with his gun, to protect his face. The pilot has an armour plate head-piece to his seat, and the back is protected from the rear and fine quarter. The underneath of the upper gunner's seat is armoured.

As the crew are well forward, they are also protected by the self-sealing fuselage fuel tank and wireless gear aft of the cabin, which would probably stop bullets from dead astern. All fuel and oil tanks are self-sealing, but there is no protection for the engines from astern or ahead.

Tactical Trials

Flying Characteristics

The Ju 88 is remarkably manoeuvrable for an aircraft of its size and wing loading. The controls are light and positive and all are assisted, with the result that they do not become heavier at high speeds but allow the aircraft to take quite violent evasion even at the end of a long dive. After gaining experience a pilot should be able to fight the aircraft quite well and give difficult deflection shooting to opposing fighters.

The Ju 88 is capable of a high top speed. In comparative trials with a Blenheim IV in which both aircraft were unladen, it appeared about 25 mph faster both at 2,000 and 15,000 feet. It accelerates quickly in a dive. The dive brakes are easily applied and are very effective. In dives of 6,000 feet at an angle of 60 degrees the maximum indicated airspeed was never more than 265 mph, and there was full control for aligning the sights. The pull-out was automatic.

The aircraft trims easily to fly hands off and instrument flying is comfortable. No night flying was carried out during the trials, but the cockpit lighting appears satisfactory by night, without reflections on the perspex. Single engined flying was carried out with each airscrew feathered in turn. The Ju 88 is not comfortable to fly on one engine but will maintain height when unladen at about 160 mph indicated. It does not turn easily against the live engine and accurate recovery from a

A Junkers 88 coming in to land on one engine. The aircraft was difficult to handle in this configuration except for the most experienced pilots. Powered by two 1,200 horse power Jumo 211D in-line engines, the Ju 88A-6 had a maximum speed of 281 mph; carrying 2,000 pounds of bombs, its effective operational radius was about 600 miles.

turn with it is difficult. It is thought, therefore, that aircraft which manage to get away after combat with only one engine intact are unlikely to be landed back in their own territory safely except by very experienced pilots.

View. The pilot's view is not good by our standards. He has to sit well up with his head almost touching the roof and even then he can see only forwards and to the port side (on which he sits) with any comfort. His view to starboard is obstructed on the bow by the front free gun and by cabin former ribs to the rear. He sits aft of the airscrews but can see over the engines more easily than in a Blenheim. The best point

about his vision is that the windscreen is made of a number of flat direct vision panels, none of which cause distortion.

The upper gunner's all-round view is good. He is of course blind beneath the wing but the lower gunner can cover the view downwards to the rear adequately. The only slightly blind spot, if the bomb aimer is not lying in position, is forward and below where sights and fittings mar the view.

Formation Flying. The Ju 88 is easy to fly in close formation, being responsive to the throttle and decelerating quite well. It is necessary, however, to be on a level with or below the leader as the engines interrupt the downward view to the sides.

Fighting Manoeuvres

General. The Ju 88 was flown in combat with Hurricane II and Spitfire I aircraft belonging to this unit. Camera guns were used by the

The Junkers 188 was developed from the Ju 88. It had more powerful engines and extended more pointed wings and an enlarged tail to improve performance at high altitude. Powered by two 1,700 horse power BMW 801 radials, the Ju 188E had a maximum speed of 310 mph; carrying 2,000 pounds of bombs, its effective operational radius was about 800 miles. *via Roosenboom*

fighters. The Ju 88 was flown without bomb loads at all times, the total weight being 22,500 pounds.

It was found that in no type of attack can the fighter be met by more than one gun at a time, and since the gun is hand-held on a gimbal mounting continuous accurate fire is very difficult. The tail-down flying attitude of the Ju 88 should always be borne in mind by fighter pilots. In level flight the tail appears to be down about 10 degrees and therefore in deflection shooting careful allowances must be made. This tail-down attitude also allows the upper gunner good shots to the rear during an astern attack.

Astern Attacks. It was found impossible for the attacking fighter to hide behind the tailplane or rudder. The upper gunner could change guns more rapidly than the fighter could move from side to side, and the lower gunner could fire at all times when the fighter went below the upper gunner's field of fire. If the attack is made on the level, the upper gunner has an easy shot due to the tail-down attitude of the Ju 88 in flight. Attacks should therefore be made just below the level of the tailplane. Since the rear of the cabin is so well armoured astern, attacks with .303-in guns should be directed at the engines which are unprotected.

The evasive manoeuvres attempted by the Ju 88 included skidding, undulating, high speed dives and turns. Of these skidding, though easy to carry out due to the light rudder, was not particularly effective and was usually detected by the fighters, but undulating caused the fighters serious sighting difficulties. The undulation was easy to effect as the Ju 88 does not lose its engines when the control column is pushed forward causing negative 'g'. The fighters found it best to remain on the top level of the undulation so as to fire at the Ju 88 at its no-deflection point and during the first part of the downward dive. The Spitfire's engine kept cutting when it tried to follow the Ju 88.

Diving appears from analysis of recent combat reports to be the favourite method of evasion adopted by the Ju 88. The Ju 88 therefore was climbed to 15,000 feet with a Spitfire and a Hurricane about a mile behind and one Hurricane as escort in formation. It then dived losing about 1,500 feet per minute at full power and the Spitfire closed up to firing range after a loss of 8,000 feet, having covered 20 miles. The attacking Hurricane, however, had closed the range only slightly. During the dive the escorting Hurricane never exceeded 4½ pounds boost pressure or 2,550 rpm. The maximum speed of the Ju 88 was 305 mph indicated. Rudder control on the Ju 88 was still very light and the tail could be swished gently to give the rear gunner a good view.

The Ju 88 also evades by means of turns, especially to gain cloud cover. It was found that it could turn quite sharply even at high speeds but the fighters never had any trouble in keeping their sights on it. However, the controls of the Ju 88 are so good that the steepness of the turns can be varied easily and side-slip added so that difficult shots are provided for the fighters.

Quarter and Beam Attacks. The Ju 88 has a little armour to protect the cabin and occupants from fine quarter attacks, so that the fighter armed with .303-in guns only must concentrate on obtaining hits during the quarter attack between 45 and 30 degrees. The upper gunner can bring his gun to bear quite easily almost on to the full beam, but the lower gunner's field of fire is only 40 degrees on each side. In addition, the lower gunner can see and fire more easily to starboard than to port and therefore attacks should be made if possible on the port quarter and from slightly below the Ju 88, and the breakaway should be downwards on the port side. A further advantage in attacking from the port is that the pilot sits on that side and is fairly exposed to quarter attacks.

Head-On Attacks. The Ju 88 is entirely unprotected from head-on attacks and with its large circular radiators presents a good target. This type of attack is ideal if the fighter can get into position unobserved, but will be impossible if he has been seen beforehand, owing to the Ju 88's high speed. The field of fire of the front gun of the Ju 88 is very limited and it is difficult to use, owing to the cramped position of the bomb aimer. His close proximity to the pilot makes firing to port easier than to starboard.

Ju 88 as a Dive Bomber. The Ju 88 was dived at angles between 50 and 60 degrees with the assistance of the dive brakes. Attacks were made by fighters from which it was found possible to fire an effective burst during the dive, before overshooting, but this prevented the fighter getting a more certain shot as the Ju 88 pulled out of the dive. It would seem best, therefore, for the fighter to spiral down during the dive and engage the Ju 88 as it pulls away. The Ju 88 also makes use of its dive brakes as a very effective evasive manoeuvre, especially when it desires to attain cloud cover.

Slipstream. The slipstream is not strong at any point. Fighters were able to come in to less than 100 yards astern and maintain quite steady bursts.

Low Flying. The Ju 88 is fully controllable

above about 160 mph and can therefore be used for low level attacks.

Night Fighter Attacks. Our fighters should normally attack from astern and below as the lower gunner's vision and arc of fire are restricted. For free-gun fighters there is a large blind spot below the centre section which can safely be approached from the beam.

De Havilland Mosquito IV

The de Havilland Mosquito IV was the first bomber version of the famous wooden aircraft (Marks I, II and III were photographic reconnaissance, fighter and trainer versions respectively). The type entered service in the spring of 1942; the trials described took place between November 1941 and March 1942, using one of the initial production aircraft.

Brief Description of the Aircraft

General

The Mosquito is a mid-wing monoplane of wooden monocoque construction, powered with two Merlin 21 engines of 1,150 hp each. The bomber version carries no armament. The present maximum all-up weight of the aircraft is 19,400 pounds. This constitutes a full load of petrol and 1,500 pounds of bombs and gives a total operational range of approximately 1,400 miles. With long-range tanks fitted in the bomb bay it is capable of about 1,800 miles.

Crew

The crew of two consists of a pilot and an observer, who also acts as bomb-aimer, radio operator and navigator.

The layout of the De Havilland Mosquito IV.

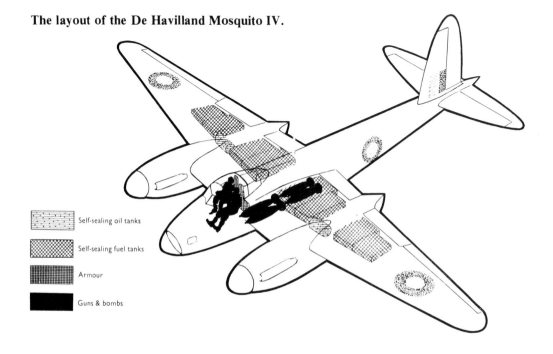

Self-sealing oil tanks

Self-sealing fuel tanks

Armour

Guns & bombs

Cockpit

The pilot's cockpit is well laid out though a trifle cramped and this together with the pilot's upright position may cause fatigue on a long flight. The various controls and instruments are well placed and easily accessible. The pilot sits on the left side and the observer normally sits beside the pilot where he carries out his duties as navigator, radio operator and look-out. The bomb sight is situated in the nose forward of the pilot and it is necessary for the observer to move into this position before bombing. A clear view panel is provided for bomb aiming. The heating of the cockpit is exceptionally good, and even in winter at altitude no bulky flying clothing need be worn. In summer the cockpit may prove to be rather too warm.

The two-man crew seen boarding a Mosquito, giving scale to this small high-speed bomber. Powered by two 1,150 horse power Rolls-Royce Merlin 21 engines, the Mosquito IV had a maximum speed of 385 mph; carrying 2,000 pounds of bombs, it had an effective operational radius of about 600 miles. *C Brown*

View

The crew have a good view above the horizontal to the sides, front and above and can see moderately well to the rear. Their view downwards and backwards, however, into the area they must search carefully is particularly bad, partly due to the blind spot and partly to the fact that both members of the crew are facing forwards and so it is difficult for them to search thoroughly when they can look only over their shoulders. On some occasions the observer knelt on his seat facing backwards and this made a certain improvement. It was found during the trials that a fighter could often approach from the rear and below without the crew being aware of its attack. Blisters are fitted to the sides of the cockpit but are difficult to use in full flying kit. Experiments were carried out with mirrors in the blisters and these were found to be a definite advantage for keeping a look-out to the rear and slightly below.

Armour

The pilot is protected from behind by armour plate of 7mm thickness, extending from the level of his seat to the top of his head. The observer is similarly protected from behind by armour plate of 9mm thickness, and there is a circular section of bullet proof glass behind his head so that his rearward view is not hindered. The upper part of the armour plate is hinged to enable the observer to operate the wireless which is behind it. There is no armour protection for the engines.

Fuel and Oil Tanks

Fuel is carried in 10 self-sealing tanks as follows:

4 Outboard wing of	118 galls
4 Inboard wing of	289 galls
2 Centre fuselage of	136 galls
	543 galls
2 Fuselage long range tanks (if fitted)	155 galls
TOTAL CAPACITY	698 galls

Oil is carried in two self-sealing tanks, one in each engine nacelle and a third can be carried in the fuselage if the long range tanks are fitted.

Bomb Load

The maximum bomb load at present is 1,500 pounds and is made up of two 500 pounders and two 250 pounders. It is understood, however, that it may be possible to increase the load to a maximum of 2,500 pounds when bombs with collapsible fins are available.

Radio

The aircraft is fitted with the standard Marconi installation for bombers which is satisfactory and the intercommunication between pilot and observer is very good.

Flying Characteristics

The Mosquito is very manoeuvrable both light and fully loaded. The controls are light and positive at all speeds, the rudder being rather heavier than the elevators or ailerons.

Performance

The Mosquito is capable of a high top speed. Comparative trials were carried out with a Spitfire VB in which both aircraft carried full operational loads. The Mosquito carried a full load of petrol and 1,000 pounds of bombs throughout the majority of the trials, though very little difference was noticed when the bombs were removed. At 21,000 feet without using emergency boost the Mosquito appeared 4 to 5 mph faster than the Spitfire which was using its emergency boost in an attempt to keep up. This gives the Mosquito a true top speed of about 375 mph. At 600 feet both aircraft attained approximately the same speed but the Spitfire was again using emergency boost while the Mosquito was not. Above 24,000 feet the performance of the Mosquito appears to fall off in comparison with the Spitfire.

The Mosquito climbs quickly, especially when light. At its maximum rate of climb it can reach 20,000 feet in just over 9 minutes from the start of the take-off run, which is only about 2½ minutes longer than the time taken by a Spitfire. The addition of bomb load does not seriously detract from its performance. The operational ceiling appears to be around 30,000 feet. When diving the Mosquito accelerates well and in a slight dive at altitude quickly reaches the limiting speed of 360 mph indicated.

Single-engine flying was carried out with each engine feathered in turn and it was found that the Mosquito can maintain height and climb comfortably on one engine, there being enough rudder trim available to enable the aircraft to be flown hands off. Again the bomb load of 1,000 pounds appears to make very little difference to the single-engined handling. Turns with and against the live engine were carried out with ease.

Instrument Flying

The blind flying panel is well placed and instrument flying is comfortable. At cruising speeds the aircraft is very stable and can be trimmed easily to fly hands off. No difficulty was experienced in night flying, the lighting being good for all essential instruments and cockpit controls without causing reflections on the cockpit hood. The exhaust flames, however, which cannot be seen from the cockpit, are rather bright when viewed from behind.

Formation Flying

No second Mosquito was available for testing the qualities of the aircraft in formation, but it is thought that this will present no difficulty. Since formation is normally resorted to only by aircraft having defensive armament in order to give mutual fire support, there is unlikely to be any need for unarmed aircraft to fly operationally in formation. This would simply present a larger target to Flak and fighters and hamper evasive action.

Fighting Manoeuvres

General

Interceptions and attacks were attempted by Spitfire V aircraft at various altitudes. If the fighter was allowed to close range, the Mosquito was unable to throw it off as its lower

The Mark XVI Mosquito, which entered service early in 1944, featured a partially-pressurized cabin, a bulged bomb bay to accommodate the 4,000lb 'Cookie' high capacity bomb, and underwing tanks for 500 Imp (60 US) gallons of fuel. *C. Brown*

safety factor of 6 does not allow sufficiently violent manoeuvring with safety. Owing to the high speed and light elevator control of the Mosquito, high acceleration forces are easily imposed but will normally be avoided as the upright position of the crew reduces the amount of 'g' that can be withstood without 'blacking out'. If the Mosquito is cruising fast, the only present-day fighters which are likely to be dangerous will have to dive down from a greater height than the Mosquito in order to attain enough speed to carry out an attack. Those that are climbing up from below will never come in range and any on the same level as the Mosquito, if seen in time, can be kept out of range if the Mosquito accelerates quickly.

Search

The Mosquito having no armament, the only tactics open to it are evasion either by speed or manoeuvrability. The key to the effectiveness of either lies in seeing the fighter in time and the view of the crew, though good forward and above the horizontal, is very blind backwards and downwards. A sharp lookout is essential at all times, especially in a danger area, and wide weaving is necessary to keep the blind spots in view as much as possible, otherwise a fighter can dive down and overtake slightly below to carry out an attack without being seen at all. It was found very difficult even with quite wide weaving to pick up a single fighter which was more than 1,000 feet below. During the trials a few successful fighter attacks were not observed at all although the crew were expecting the attacks, due partly to the blind spot and partly to the difficulty of searching thoroughly in any direction other than that in which they were facing. In particular when approaching the target area, when the observer is over the bomb sight, the pilot must try to cover the whole area of search behind and below by himself. This difficult task was eased considerably by adjusting the mirror fitted in the starboard blister to help in covering the starboard quarter.

High Altitude

The best performance of the Mosquito being obtained at 21,000 feet, the majority of altitude interceptions and attacks were carried out at or just above this height. The Mosquito being superior in speed to the Spitfire at all heights below about 24,000 feet, its best evasion was by accelerating away and preventing the fighter coming into range. If the Spitfire attacked with a 3,000 foot advantage, the Mosquito was never able to accelerate enough from fast cruising to prevent the Spitfire from diving down below and getting in a burst of fire of fairly long duration from astern. But if the Spitfire was only about 2,000 feet above and 1,000 yards away on the beam, the Mosquito could get away. In each case the Mosquito's acceleration was helped by its going into a slight dive. It appears therefore that the best operating height is one that is above 21,000 feet, to allow the Mosquito to accelerate in a dive down to its rated altitude.

During these trials the Mosquito had to weave and turn as soon as the Spitfire dived down behind and below in order to keep it in view, and it attempted evasion by means of turning when the fighter came into range. This was not particularly effective as the Mosquito could not go into a turn at high speed which was violent enough to throw the fighter off or upset his aim unduly at short range.

As an alternative, when the Spitfire was coming into range the Mosquito attempted a corkscrewing movement, diving about 500 feet in a turn and recovering by a climb and turn in the opposite direction. During the first attempts the engines cut badly at the top of this manoeuvre when the aircraft was put into a dive and the movement was hardly violent enough to be effective. RAE type restrictors as fitted to Merlin XX and 45 engines in Fighter Command were placed in the fuel supply pipe lines and gave a great improvement, preventing the cutting of the engines under 'negative g' and making the manoeuvre quite effective. At high speed, pilots found it uncomfortable to make sudden movements in the fore and aft plane and at heights above about 20,000 feet it felt as if this evasion was so slight that it was not putting the fighter off his aim. In actual fact it has been found that very slight movements by a target travelling at high speed forces a fighter pilot to allow conderable deflection and this form of evasion, even at altitude, usually prevented the fighter from taking an accurate aim. Since the fighter on occasion was able to remain in range dead astern for a considerable period, this evasion was found necessary and more effective for upsetting his aim at long range than an attempt to turn. It had the added advantage of allowing the Mosquito to remain more or less on its original course.

Medium Altitude

The Mosquito's performance at low altitudes still being superior to that of the Spitfire, similar results were obtained at the rated altitude for the 'M' Supercharger, ie about 15,000 feet, but the corkscrewing movement was easier to carry out at this height. If the Mosquito therefore is unable to operate as high as 21,000 feet it should try to fly slightly above 15,000 feet in order to benefit from the acceleration picked up in a dive down to the lower rated altitude.

Low Altitude

Trials were also carried out below 1,000 feet in a similar way to those at altitude and with similar results. The Mosquito had a far better chance of spotting fighters as they were usually attacking from above and if seen in time it could always accelerate away. The forward view from the Mosquito being extremely good, low flying can be carried out quite easily and with practice fairly steep turns and evasive manoeuvres can be carried out at high speed. Such turns provided more effective evasion than at altitude but even so the fighter if in close range was presented with a fairly easy shot. The corkscrewing manoeuvre, however, could be carried out far more easily than at altitude and was the more effective, especially as the fighter was frequently forced into the slipstream which he found particularly uncomfortable near the ground.

Effects of Opening the Bomb Doors

The reduction in speed caused by opening the bomb doors and the time to open and close were noted, and attacks were carried out on the Mosquito with the bomb doors open. It was found that at a high cruising speed the Mosquito lost about 20 mph over a period of 3 minutes by opening the bomb doors. The doors opened in 13 seconds and closed in 11 seconds and the time taken to accelerate back to the original speed was approximately 30 seconds from the commencement of closing. During the attacks which were subsequently carried out at 24,000 feet, it was found that the Mosquito could just keep out of range of a fighter seen for instance 2,000 feet above and 1,200 yards away if the bomb doors were closed immediately and the Mosquito accelerated in a slight dive. During attacks carried out at 1,000 feet, however, the doors had to be closed while the fighter was much further away, as it was impossible for the Mosquito to dive far to gain speed.

Evasion by Climbing

The rate of climb of the Mosquito being so good, a few attacks were carried out while it flew between 1,000 and 2,000 feet below cloud. Unless the fighter was allowed to get nearer than 1,000 yards, the Mosquito had no trouble in gaining cloud cover.

Slipstream

The slipstream behind the Mosquito covers only a very small area and is encountered on the level, being most noticeable slightly to port. Though strong from 400 yards inwards, it did not disturb the fighters except when the Mosquito was at very low altitude and corkscrewing, when they flew into it frequently and found difficulty in sighting. At 600 yards and over its effects were negligible.

The Avro Lancaster I

The Lancaster entered service early in 1942 and rapidly became the most important heavy bomber type used by the Royal Air Force. The trials described took place during April and May 1942.

Brief Description of the Aircraft

General

The Lancaster I is a mid-wing monoplane powered with four Merlin XX engines developing 1,280 hp each. The present gross all-up weight is 60,200 pounds, and the maximum bomb load carried at present is 12,000 pounds, though there is provision for carrying 14,000 pounds when necessary. With 12,000 pounds of bombs the total air mileage that can be covered is 1,100 to 1,200 miles. The maximum air mileage available is about 2,000 miles, in which case the bomb load must be reduced to 4,000 pounds.

Crew

The crew consists of seven whose duties are as follows:

Captain and Second Pilot	— At controls
Air Observer	— Navigator and Bomb Aimer
1st Wireless Operator/ Air Gunner	— At wireless
2nd Wireless Operator/ Air Gunner	— Front turret
Air Gunner	— Mid-upper turret
Air Gunner	— Tail turret

It is understood, however, that the second pilot will shortly be replaced by the pilot's assistant, who will aid the pilot and also act as flight engineer and front gunner. An air bomber whose duties are map reading and bombing will be carried in place of a second wireless operator.

Wireless and Inter-Communication

The standard bomber wireless installation is carried. The TR 9 for intercommunication has proved fairly satisfactory, but a very high standard of maintenance is necessary if this is to be relied on for formation fighting control.

De-icing Equipment

De-icers are provided for the propellers but there is no protection for the main or tail planes other than de-icing paste.

Balloon Cutters

Balloon [cable] cutters are fitted along the leading edge of the mainplane.

The layout of the Avro Lancaster I.

▥	Dural deflector plates
▤	Self-sealing oil tanks
▨	Self-sealing fuel tanks
▦	Armour
■	Guns & bombs

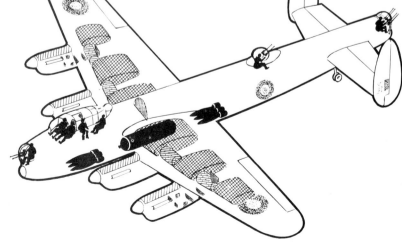

Armament Characteristics

General

The Lancaster is at present armed with .303-in Browning guns in three Frazer-Nash turrets. The FN 5A in the nose and the FN 50 in the dorsal position have two guns each, with an ammunition supply of 1,000 rounds per gun. The FN 20 in the tail has four guns with a servo-feed mechanism and 2,500 rounds per gun.

Front Turret

The FN 5A in the nose has a good field of view and is satisfactory in all respects except that there is no foot rest for the gunner. This is extremely inconvenient when the bomb aimer is in position as the gunner is liable to tread on the bomb-aimer's head in moments of stress.

Mid-upper Turret

The FN 50 in the dorsal position is a comfortable and roomy turret, although the seat design is unsatisfactory. This results in the gunner having great difficulty in entering or leaving the turret. The field of vision is very good and attacks can be seen from any angle except a very steep climbing attack from dead astern. The turret has rotation through 360 degrees and its movement when the guns are elevated about 20 degrees is fast and smooth. Cut-outs are provided for the tail fins and a taboo cam track runs round the turret to prevent damage to the wings, propellers and the tail unit. A restrictor valve is fitted to the hydraulic system to slow down the movement of the guns when they are depressed on to the taboo cam so that a violent movement does not damage the fuselage or fairings. This restriction, however, is not at all satisfactory since the movement of the guns is slowed down so much that it is impossible to follow a fighter who breaks away at fairly close range. As this is usually the air gunner's best opportunity to shoot down the fighter, the loss of rotational speed at this critical moment is serious. While some restriction is clearly necessary, it is considered that the present reduction in speed is too great for reasonable operational requirements. The fairing which has been

introduced aft of the turret for streamlining purposes is also too high, as the cam track which runs over it cuts down the field of fire between the fuselage and the fins considerably.

Tail Turret

The FN 20 turret in the tail is satisfactory and accurate, and fast traversing is possible. The vision is naturally somewhat restricted by the armour and gun mountings, but it is impossible to have armour and perfect vision, and a reasonable compromise has been effected. Unless the base of the turret is kept perfectly dry, oil is liable to be forced up the rear perspex by the slipstream, but a clear vision panel 6 inches wide by 30 inches long has much improved the position. This makes the gunner very cold under icing conditions, but the extra vision and reduction of searchlight glare more than compensate for the discomfort. One other minor criticism of this turret is that the doors are liable to burst open when taking violent evasion as the locking catch is not sufficiently positive.

Sights

The GJ 3 reflector sight is fitted to all turrets.

Harmonisation

The four guns of the rear turret are harmonised on a point at 250 yards at night and on a 7'6" square by day. The upper and front guns are usually harmonised 5 feet apart at 400 yards.

Armour

Apart from the normal turret armour for the air gunners, the main protection for the crew consists of an armoured door 7mm thick behind the wireless operator's position. The pilot also has two plates of armour, each of 4mm thickness, behind his seat and a head piece of 8½mm. Bullet proof glass 60mm thick is provided behind the second pilot's position. The petrol and oil tanks are self-sealing but the engines have no protection.

Tactical Trials

Flying Characteristics

The Lancaster is reasonably manoeuvrable for a large aircraft. The controls are positive and moderately heavy under normal cruising conditions, but tend to stiffen appreciably as speed is increased over 200 mph. When any evasive manoeuvres are attempted, however, there is a considerable lag in the aileron control and this is very marked when the aircraft is fully loaded. This means that considerable practice is required before violent evasion is possible at ground level. The cruising speed is approximately 185 mph indicated with full load and about 220 mph indicated when light. The maximum speed near the ground at a weight of 60,000 pounds is approximately 220 mph indicated.

Fields of View and Fighting Control

The combined all-round view from the Lancaster is good. Owing to the raised position of the cabin the pilot's general view, although slightly restricted on the starboard side, is satisfactory towards the beam and quarter, and of considerable assistance in taking evasive action. The fighting controller can stand just behind the second pilot but this gives a poor view downwards and even if he uses the astro-hatch beside the wireless operator, he is still given a large blind area by the main-plane. For this reason control is mainly carried out by the mid-upper gunner who is able to see all attacks except those from beneath and directly astern. For these he relies on the rear gunner so that with practice a good commentary can easily be maintained.

It is considered, however, that it is a mistake for air gunners to carry out fighting control as it is extremely difficult to combine control with good shooting. If, therefore, a low level sortie is to be made, with the result that attacks must develop from above, the fighting control should be carried out from the astro-hatch.

Fighting Manoeuvres for Single Aircraft

General. The trials were carried out with the object of discovering the best method of evasion by the Lancaster against all types of attack both by single fighters or by a number of fighters simultaneously. It has already been found in previous trials with heavy bombers

that the only really effective evasion against the astern, quarter or beam attacks is the corkscrew, or the tight turn towards the fighter. Other forms of evasion, such as skidding, undulation and throttling back are useful but not so effection.

Corkscrew. This form of evasion consists of a steep diving turn of about 30 degrees and 500 feet, followed by a steep climbing turn of 30 degrees and 500 feet in the opposite direction. The manoeuvre must be as violent as possible, particularly at the top and bottom of the corkscrew, to avoid giving an easy deflection shot. It should begin when the first fighter attacking is at 600 yards and should be continued throughout the engagement unless all the fighters attacking can clearly be seen by the controller to be out of position, when normal flight can be resumed. This evasion is tiring for the pilot and must be stopped immediately it is clear that no immediate attacks are developing. The main advantages of corkscrewing are that the bomber can make good its course, while the fighter is given difficult deflection in two dimensions in that he has to aim in front and below during the diving turn, and in front and above during the climb. Assessment of fighters' cine camera gun films proved in the case of the Lancaster, as with other four-engined bombers, that even the most experienced fighter pilots who knew what the evasion was to be were able to obtain only moderate results. Height can be maintained without any extra throttle opening when the Lancaster is without bomb load, but when fully loaded slight opening is necessary to regain height in the climbing turn. This evasion does not affect the air gunners' shooting as much as a tight turn and did not prevent their obtaining good cine camera gun results when they became used to the movement.

A 'Vic' formation of Lancasters of No 207 Squadron, Royal Air Force. Powered by four 1,280 horse power Rolls-Royce Merlin XX engines, this bomber had a maximum speed of 270 mph; carrying maximum normal fuel, the bomb load was 4,000 pounds for an effective operational radius of about 875 miles. *C. Brown*

Tight Turn. The Lancaster is sufficiently manoeuvrable to be able to do a very tight turn and, if this is timed correctly, a fighter who is making an attack at a fast overtaking speed is given difficult deflection and only a short burst of fire. Against a steep diving attack, a slightly climbing turn is advisable but against a normal astern attack, a diving turn is best as it enables the Lancaster to gain speed. Both of these manoeuvres increase the fighter's deflection. The tight turn is the best evasion against a single fighter provided that it is correctly timed — at about 600 yards — and that there is no question of shortage of petrol or other fighters coming up to engage the bomber. Under the latter circumstances or if more than one fighter is attacking, the corkscrew evasive manoeuvre is more effective, because it enables the bomber to maintain a course and height instead of flying in circles.

Head-On Attacks. Head-on attacks were carried out against the Lancaster but were difficult to deliver owing to its high speed. It is often possible for the Lancaster to prevent the attack developing by edging towards the fighter when it is trying to get into position. If the attack is delivered, a diving turn at about 800 yards is effective and gives the fighter an extremely difficult deflection allowance. The mid-upper gunner, who will be facing forwards for this type of attack, is given a reasonable shot.

Fighting Manoeuvres for Formations

Low Level Attacks. It is considered that a formation of more than three Lancasters is unwieldy if adequate individual evasive action is to be taken. The three aircraft should be in Vic formation with Nos 2 and 3 only slightly behind the leader and at about 1½ wing spans interval. The leader can fly at about 50 feet with Nos 2 and 3 slightly above, to give them a small margin if the leader has to climb up suddenly to avoid ground obstacles.

Fighter affiliation exercises carried out by the squadrons have proved that if a formation of Lancasters simply relies upon low flying, it will always provide an easy target for fighters. If the formation is intercepted it should therefore climb to about 600 to 700 feet. This is absolutely essential to give the bombers room to manoeuvre. It cannot be over-emphasised that flying at ground level is not in itself an adequate form of evasion when attacked.

In the past it has usually been considered that tight turns in formation are the best form of defence against fighters but it is almost impossible with heavy bombers to make the turns sufficiently steep to upset the fighters' aim. Turns also have another very serious defect as they have to be begun early in order to make them at all effective, and this results in the formation turning through nearly 180 degrees. It can be seen that a series of turns results in the bombers flying in circles so that they waste petrol and are unable to maintain their track towards the target.

It has also been found in the majority of recent daylight operations that the German fighters are shy of the power-operated turrets and stand off at 400 to 600 yards using their cannon. The result is that if any close formation is adopted by the bombers they present a mass target while adding nothing to their mutual fire support, owing to the limited effective range of their .303-in ammunition.

It has therefore been necessary to develop a form of evasive action which will give the bombers a chance to carry out individual evasion while maintaining their track to the target and giving each other assistance. Just before the fighters attack, the Lancasters should climb up to about 600 feet and numbers 2 and 3 should come well up on the beam of the leader. When the fighters close in, the leader of the Vic should undulate violently between 600 feet and ground level, while Nos 2 and 3 carry out a modified form of corkscrew on either side of the leader, beginning with a diving turn outwards of about 20 degrees and varying their height between 600 and 1,000 feet. Practice is necessary to ensure that the outside aircraft are never more than 300 to 400 yards from the leader and that they do not mask his guns by sliding in behind him during their inward movement. Nos 2 and 3 should attempt to keep as close as possible to the leader until an attack actually develops so that during their evasion

A Lancaster carrying the 22,000-pound 'Grand Slam', the largest type of bomb to be used in action during the war. To enable it to carry this weapon the Lancaster had to be extensively modified, with the nose and mid-upper gun turrets removed. Carrying the 'Grand Slam', the Lancaster had an effective operational radius of about 650 miles. *Garbett/Goulding*

they will not go too far away from him. This evasive manoeuvre enables the formation to continue upon track while it gives the fighters difficult deflection shooting. The fighters found it hard to attack the leader as he was protected by the guns of the outside aircraft, and if they followed an outside aircraft in its corkscrew they were soon drawn under the leader's guns. A further advantage of this manoeuvre is that the slipstream of the formation is fanned out over a large area and frequently upsets the fighters' aim, being particularly unpleasant near the ground. This form of evasion has been tried by nearly all the squadrons of heavy bombers and has proved very satisfactory under practice conditions.

Fighting Control. An advantage of the formation corkscrew movement is that fighting control by the leader is not essential. It is still necessary so that the leader can warn Nos 2 and 3 when he wishes to change course, but with the present standard of radio equipment and maintenance it is not advisable to rely absolutely on TR 9 control.

High Level Attacks. Little high level formation flying has yet been attempted. It is considered that the corkscrew evasion described for low level attacks will again be effective and would be useful against Flak prior to the actual bombing run. It is thought, however, that fighting control from the leader would be essential, so that the formation could have time to settle down preparatory to bombing.

Night Flying

A short night flight was carried out with a fighter observing the exhaust flames from the Lancaster; there was no moon and 10/10ths cloud. The flames appear as a very dim glow and can be seen from about 500 yards dead astern. On closing range they appeared rather like eight bright cigarette ends, at about 150 to 200 yards. The exhausts are not visible from any position other than dead astern and at long ranges are unlikely to catch the eye of a night fighter pilot until he is looking directly at them.

Slipstream

The slipstream of the Lancaster is fairly strong at the same level as the aircraft back to 600 yards, but is only of real tactical value at about 400 yards where it is sufficiently vicious to upset a fighter's aim completely.

The Consolidated Liberator II

The Liberator Mark II was the first version of the aircraft to serve as a bomber. A total of 139 examples were built for the Royal Air Force and the type entered service early in 1942. The trials described took place in April 1942.

The Liberator II served as a bomber only in the RAF and had no US Army Air Force equivalent. The first bomber version of the Liberator to enter large scale production for the USAAF was the B-24D, which differed from the Liberator II in having turbo-supercharged engines, the dorsal turret moved to a position just aft of the cockpit, and .5-in guns in all positions. In general, however, the report's comments apply to the USAAF versions of this aircraft also.

Brief Description of the Aircraft

General

The Liberator II is a high-wing monoplane powered with four Pratt and Whitney Twin Wasp engines of 1,200 hp each. It is fitted with a tricycle undercarriage, hydraulically operated, with the main wheels retracting outwards into the wings. The nose wheel, which is free to swivel when under load, is automatically aligned in the fore and aft position in flight; it retracts behind the observer's compartment. The fuselage is of light alloy monocoque construction divided into the following four compartments:

Nose Compartment where the observer carries

The layout of the Consolidated B-24J Liberator.

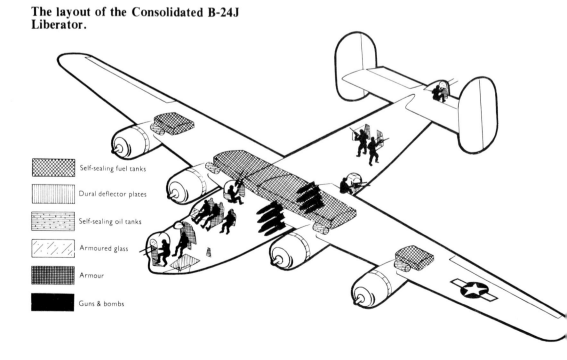

- Self-sealing fuel tanks
- Dural deflector plates
- Self-sealing oil tanks
- Armoured glass
- Armour
- Guns & bombs

out his duties of navigator and bomb aimer and which is provided with an astro-hatch.

Pilots' Cockpit with permanent dual control for the 1st and 2nd pilots who are seated beside one another. They are separated by a pedestal on which are mounted all the engine and subsidiary controls.

Bomb Compartment with a catwalk connecting the cockpit with the rear of the fuselage.

Rear Compartment with positions for the mid-upper and tail turrets, beam and under-gun installations.

The present gross all-up weight of the aircraft is 56,000 pounds. The maximum endurance without additional tanks and with a full bomb load of 8,000 pounds is approximately 2,200 miles. A reduction of the bomb load does not increase range appreciably.

Crew

The crew at present consists of seven, whose duties are as follows:

1st and 2nd Pilots	— At controls
Air Observer	— Navigator and bomb aimer
1st Wireless Operator/ Air Gunner	— Wireless and under gunner
2nd Wireless Operator/ Air Gunner	— Wireless and beam gunner
Air Gunner	— Mid-upper turret
Air Gunner	— Tail turret

A fighting controller will probably be carried on daylight operations.

Emergency Exits

The main exits in flight are the under-gun position for those in the rear compartment and through the bomb bays for the remainder of the crew. The bomb doors, which open electrically, slide in grooves up the side of the fuselage and are automatically opened before bombs are jettisoned, the whole operation taking under 10 seconds. In the event of a crash landing, additional exits are provided in the top of the pilots' and observer's compartments and though the openings for the beam guns. For ditching, two dinghies are released by a handle behind the 2nd wireless operator's seat.

Armament Characteristics

General

The main armament consists of Boulton and Paul tail and mid-upper turrets with four guns in each. There is also a twin gun installation on each side of the fuselage and single guns in the nose and in the belly of the aircraft. All guns are .303-in Brownings.

Mid-upper Turret

The mid-upper turret is the A Mk IV armed with 600 rounds per gun, with spare tanks of similar capacity. It has a rotation of 360 degrees and elevation of 84 degrees but no depression. Automatic cut-outs are provided to prevent damage to the tail, propellers and astro-hatch. The turret is very efficient and smooth in action even when turning into the slipstream. There is a gap between the fuselage and the turret and although this is not large it is sufficient to let in the rain and also to make the turret extremely draughty. This draught is so great that the noise makes intercommunication difficult and the cold would be unbearable for more than 1 or 2 hours under freezing conditions. A modification is believed to be in hand to reduce the size of the gap by a form of rubber flange. The field of view is fair, although it is poor on the quarter owing to the size of the twin tail fins.

Tail Turret

The tail turret is the E Mk II with servo-feed mechanism and 2,200 rounds per gun. This will be increased to 2,500 rounds per gun when modified belts are available. The turret is comfortable and efficient in operation and has a rotation of 65 degrees each side of the central position. It has an elevation of 60 degrees and a depression of 50 degrees. The view is moderately good but restricted by the perspex frames which are rather wide, and by the tail fins which blot out the beam area.

Beam Guns

These were not fitted to the aircraft with which the trials were carried out, but are understood to be twin Brownings with parallel linkage, with belts of 1,000 rounds per gun.

Nose and Belly Guns

These are free guns in gimbal mountings with an ammunition supply of five magazines of 100 rounds each. Their field of fire is limited and they are mainly of value for scare purposes.

Sights

The GJ3 reflector sight is fitted in the turrets and beam gun positions, and the G1 prismatic sight is provided for the two free guns.

Harmonisation

The four guns in the mid-upper and tail turrets are harmonised on a 7′6″ square at 400 yards.

Armour

The seats of the pilots and wireless operators are protected from the rear by shaped pieces of armour plate of 6mm and 8mm thickness respectively. Two shields of 6mm thickness are provided just aft of the beam gunner's position. The mid-upper and tail gunners have the usual Boulton and Paul design of face and chest armour. The petrol tanks are self-sealing but the oil tanks and engines have no protection.

De-icing Equipment

The propellers are provided with de-icers and rubber pulsators are fitted on the leading edge of the mainplane and tail unit, and are believed to be very satisfactory.

The Consolidated Liberator II, described in detail in the text, saw service only in the Royal Air Force and was not supplied to the US Army Air Force. Powered by four 1,200 horse power Pratt and Whitney Twin Wasp radials, it had a maximum speed of 263 mph; carrying 8,000 pounds of bombs, it had an effective operational radius of about 1,000 miles. *IWM*

Tactical Trials

Flying Characteristics

The Liberator II is very manoeuvrable for an aircraft of its size. The controls, though heavy, are very positive and do not stiffen noticeably at high speeds. The normal operational height with full bomb load is between 12,000 feet and 15,000 feet and at these heights in weak mixture, economical cruising gives a true speed of approximately 210 to 215 mph. A speed of about 225 mph can however be maintained without serious loss of range and the true maximum speed is in the neighbourhood of 250 mph.

Fields of View and Fighting Control

The pilots' view forward and above is good, but is rather restricted to the sides and rear. Blisters are fitted to the sliding panels beside the pilots' heads, but these are inclined to mist up and also cause refraction. The astro-hatch provided for fighting control is liable to mist up on the inside. It is understood that a modification is in hand by which a current of air is directed on to the inside surface of the hatch so that the temperature remains constant. Owing to the fact that the Liberator flies in a distinctly tail-up attitude and the astro-hatch is forward of the leading edge of the mainplane, the view below the line of the fuselage is very poor and it is therefore necessary for the tail gunner to act as controller when attacked from below. This needs a very high standard of co-operation between the tail gunner and fighting controller and in fact among the whole crew, as the upper gunner and navigator may often see beam attacks from below which are invisible to the others. The crux of the matter is that all the crew have a limited view and that considerable practice is absolutely essential to give an adequate commentary to the pilot and to prevent congestion on the intercom.

Fighting Manoeuvres for Single Aircraft

General. The trials were carried out with the object of discovering the best method of evasion by the Liberator against all types of attack, both by single fighters or by a number of fighters simultaneously. It has already been found in previous trials with heavy bombers that the only really effective evasion against astern, quarter or beam attacks is the tight turn towards the fighter or the corkscrew. Other forms of evasion such as skidding, undulating and throttling back are useful, but not as effective.

Tight Turn. The Liberator is sufficiently manoeuvrable to be able to do a very tight turn and, if it is timed correctly, a fighter who is making an attack at a fast overtaking speed is given difficult deflection and only a short burst of fire. Against a diving attack, a slightly climbing turn is advisable but against a normal astern attack, a diving turn is best as it enables the Liberator to gain speed. Both these manoeuvres increase the fighter's deflection. The tight turn is the best evasive manoeuvre against a single fighter provided that it is correctly timed — at about 600 yards — and that there is no question of shortage of petrol or

other fighters coming up to engage the bomber. Under the latter circumstances or if more than one fighter is attacking, the corkscrew evasion is more effective, because it enables the bomber to maintain a course and height instead of flying in circles.

Corkscrew. This form of evasion consists of a diving turn of about 30 degrees and 500 feet, followed by a steep climbing turn of 30 degrees and 500 feet in the opposite direction. The manoeuvre must be as violent as possible, particularly at the top and bottom of the corkscrew. It should begin when the first fighter attacking is at 600 yards and should be continued throughout the engagement unless all the fighters attacking can be clearly seen by the controller to be out of position, when the normal course can be resumed. Although this evasion is tiring for the pilot it must not be stopped when one fighter has attacked and broken away, as the combined view of the crew is not good enough to ensure that the Liberator is not surprised from below. The main advantages of corkscrewing are that the bomber can make good its course, while the fighter is given difficult deflection in two directions in that he has to aim in front and below during the diving turn and in front and above during the climb. Assessment of fighters' cine camera gun films proved in the case of the Liberator as with other four-engined bombers that even the most experienced fighter pilots who knew what the evasion was to be, were unable to obtain good results. The Liberator is a suitable aircraft for this manoeuvre as the engines, which have Stromberg carburettors, do not cut when the nose is pushed down again at the top of the climbing turn. Height can be maintained without any extra throttle opening. This evasion does not affect the gunners' shooting as much as a tight turn, and did not prevent them from obtaining good cine camera gun results. Although the upper turret has no depression, this does not handicap the gunner during any violent evasion such as the tight turn or the corkscrew, because the aircraft is at a sufficient bank to give all the depression needed

In time of war, the finest bomber design is of little value unless it can be produced in sufficient numbers. Mass production became the order of the day, and the Americans excelled at it. This photograph shows the world's first moving production line for heavy bombers, at the Consolidated Vultee plant at San Diego, California. B-24J Liberators were moving down the line at 8½ inches per minute; between 1941 and 1945 the plant turned out more than 6,500 of these bombers. Altogether, a total of more than eighteen thousand Liberator bombers were built, a vastly greater number than any other heavy bomber type. *Consolidated*

against a fighter making a steep climbing attack.

As the view from the Liberator is not good downwards and it is protected from above by the upper turret, it is probable that enemy fighter attacks will come from below. In this case it is advisable for the Liberator to increase its cruising speed and so make attacks from below more difficult to time. The increase in boost and revs to obtain this maximum cruising speed for an engagement lasting 30 minutes does not increase the petrol consumption very drastically and reduces the range only by about 50 miles. Corkscrewing was no more difficult at the higher speed and resulted in the fighter's deflection allowances being increased considerably. In fact, during any engagement when the Liberator is not working at its maximum range, a reasonable increase in speed is advisable provided that a speed of not more than about 190 mph indicated is maintained. The increased speed also reduces the number of attacks which the fighters can make.

Head-On Attacks. Head-on attacks were carried out against the Liberator but were difficult to deliver owing to its high speed. It is often possible for the Liberator to prevent the attack developing by edging towards the fighter when it is trying to get into position. If the attack is delivered, a diving turn of about 800 yards is effective and gives the fighter a very difficult deflection allowance. The mid-upper gunner, who will be facing forwards for this type of attack, is given a reasonable shot.

Fighting Manoeuvres for Formations

Owing to the fact that only two modified aircraft were available for the trials and that no formation flying had previously been attempted, it was not possible to reach any very definite conclusions upon the types of formation likely to prove satisfactory. The Liberator is undoubtedly tiring for formation work as the controls — in particular the elevators — are heavy. It was possible to maintain formation one wing-span apart for short periods, but for any length of time or for evasive action, a distance of at least two wing-spans would be necessary.

Attacks were carried out by fighters and turns were attempted under the control of the leader. A bank of 30 to 40 degrees was possible and this was sufficient to give the upper turrets enough depression to bring their guns to bear on fighters attacking from below. It is considered that a formation of three aircraft in Vic or four aircraft in Box could carry out reasonable turns satisfactorily with a little practice. The main difficulty however lies in the fighting control. The view is so restricted from any individual aircraft that if the evasive turns are left to the leader he will probably fail to see an attack on other aircraft in the formation, particularly if it is from below. If the formation relies on control from any aircraft, congestion occurs and No 2 and No 3 might give orders to turn at the same time in opposite directions, when a number of fighters attack simultaneously. On the other hand, if no evasive action is taken and the Liberators rely entirely on their fire power, the upper guns cannot be brought to bear on attacks from below owing to their lack of depression. It therefore appears that unless sufficient practice can be given to all the crews in a formation so that their joint fighting control is perfect, evasive action by turns is liable to lead to many attacks being delivered unseen without any adequate manoeuvre in reply.

One solution to this problem is a form of evasive action which has been adopted by other heavy bombers with success in exercises with fighters. A Box formation is used with No 4 as close to the leader as possible, but stepped down so that he does not mask the tail guns. No 2 and No 3 start to corkscrew gently when the enemy fighters attack, going up and down 200 to 300 feet and never being more than 300 yards from the leader. They are thus able to bring all their guns to bear and to give the fighter difficult deflection, while still receiving fire support from the leader and No 4. The fighters found that it was very difficult to time their attacks in such a way that they got a burst at the corkscrewing aircraft and yet remained out of range of the guns of the rest of the formation. The leader can maintain his course and should attempt no evasion other than very slight weaving or undulating, if about to be attacked. This manoeuvre has proved comparatively simple to execute after a little practice in corkscrewing has been carried out. This formation combines the use of joint fire power with reasonably effective evasion for the outside aircraft, who normally bear the brunt of the fighter attacks. It has the advantage that it needs no control and also it enables the leader to maintain his course.

Low Flying

The Liberator is considered to be suitable for low flying over an area not heavily defended by Flak owing to its high speed and manoeuvrability. This has the added advantage of preventing fighter attacks from below. It will also result in fighters having to make their breakaway upwards or to the beam and this gives the upper and tail turrets an easy shot. The best evasion at low altitude is to climb to about 800 feet when the fighters are out of range, and then to corkscrew. The slipstream is sufficiently strong to make fighter attacks unpleasant at ground level.

Night Flying

No attacks were carried out by night on a Liberator as the flame dampers had not been fitted. The dampers are understood to be satisfactory and are very necessary as the exhaust flames of the unmodified aircraft can be seen from the ground when the aircraft is at 8,000 feet on a dark night. Experience with other heavy bombers has shown that the best evasion for all such types by night is the diving turn or spiral on a dark night, with the corkscrew as the alternative during the full moon period.

Slipstream

The slipstream tends to rise slightly and is fairly strong up to 300 yards. It is not considered to be of much tactical value although it sometimes makes accurate shooting at close range difficult, particularly at ground level.

The North American B-25C, which served in the Royal Air Force as the Mitchell II. The unsatisfactory periscopically sighted ventral turret is shown in the retracted position. *C Brown*

The North American B-25C (Mitchell II)

The B-25 entered service with the US Army Air Corps in mid-1941. Early in 1942 deliveries began of the B-25C, the first version of this bomber to go into large-scale production. This type served in the Royal Air Force as the Mitchell II and the trials described took place in September and October 1942. The B-25 became the most-used medium bomber type in the US Army Air Force and also served in large numbers with the US Navy, the RAF and the Soviet Air Force.

Brief Description of the Aircraft

General

The Mitchell (B-25C) is a fully cantilever mid-wing monoplane with twin rudders and tricycle undercarriage. It is powered by two Double Cyclone engines developing 1,600 hp each. The gross all-up weight is 29,000 pounds and the maximum bomb load at present is 4,000 pounds.

The crew at present numbers four, consisting of a pilot, navigator/bomb aimer, upper gunner and wireless operator/under gunner. There is provision for a second pilot with complete dual control. The aircraft is divided into three main compartments with tunnel communication between them. The front compartment has a position in the nose for the Mark IX bombsight and vision for bombing is good. There is a seat for the bomb aimer and a free gun position. The pilot's cockpit is very well laid out with complete dual flying controls. The engine and ancillary controls are mounted on a pedestal in the central position and can be reached equally well from either seat. The pilot's view in every direction is exceptionally good but there is no clear vision panel, with the result that in rain the view is bad and landing is extremely difficult. The navigator's seat and chart table are in the well behind the pilot's cockpit and he is equipped with a drift sight and astro-dome. The rear compartment has positions for the mid-upper gunner and the wireless operator. The latter mans the under turret and is also responsible for the camera and flare positions which are aft of the rear entry hatch. There is a look-out position in the tail of the aircraft, but it is unlikely that this will be manned as it will entail carrying an additional crew member. The

Layout of the B-25D Mitchell.

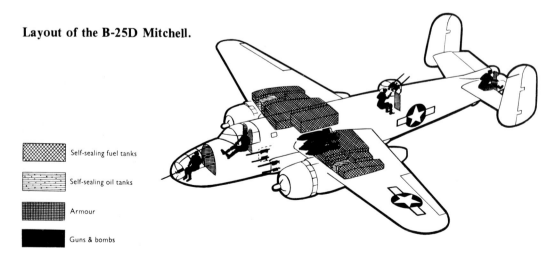

Self-sealing fuel tanks

Self-sealing oil tanks

Armour

Guns & bombs

position is tiring as it is necessary to lie face downwards and the vibration is considerable.

Wireless and Intercommunication

Standard American Bendix wireless equipment is installed with a separate interphone unit with larynx type microphones. This has proved satisfactory although it is necessary for the upper gunner to fix the earphones into a normal RAF helmet to overcome the extraneous noise when the turret is rotated on the beam. It is also difficult for the upper gunner to hold down the press button to transmit and a handle has therefore been made with the press-button attached. This handle also enables the gunner to hold himself firmly in position when the aircraft is taking evasive action.

Heating Equipment

Cabin heating is provided by the Stewart Warner system of hot air ducts to all crew positions. At low temperatures with all ducts open the heating is not sufficient but sockets are provided for electrically heated clothing for all crew members.

Oxygen

The normal American low pressure oxygen system is fitted and is considered satisfactory.

Emergency Exits

The two entry hatches, which are behind the pilot's controls and behind the armoured door of the rear compartment, have emergency quick release handles and are the normal parachute exits. For exit after ditching there is an escape hatch in the roof of the pilot's cockpit and a small window in the side of the rear compartment. The dinghy is stowed on the port side of the fuselage and can be released internally or externally by the rear gunner.

Armament Characteristics

General

The Mitchell is at present armed with Bendix all-electric turrets in the mid-upper and under positions, with two .5-in Browning guns in each. There is a .3-in Browning in a gimbal mounting in the nose.

Upper Turret

The turret has full rotation through 360 degrees and the guns, which have an ammunition supply of 430 rounds each, have a maximum elevation of 80 degrees but no depression. Cut-outs are provided to prevent damage to the tail unit, mainplanes and propellers. A periscopic sight was originally fitted but this had to be removed owing to its bulky size and small eye freedom. A mounting for a GJ 3 reflector sight is being produced by the Bristol Aeroplane Company and this should greatly improve the turret from the operational point of view. The field of view from the turret is excellent as the gun mountings and structural supports for the cupola are well below the gunner's line of sight and the plexiglass is of a very high standard. The view downwards on the beam and quarter is good and a fighter is hidden by the tail only when below and almost dead astern.

The turret controls are poor judged by RAF standards, as they are too sensitive at low speeds and barely fast enough at high speeds. A new cam has been designed by the A & AEE Boscombe Down which will improve the control, but it is considered that the turret could be used operationally in its present condition as soon as the new sight is fitted, provided the gunners receive sufficient practice in turret manipulation. The gunner's position is rather cramped and, as already stated, a handle is necessary for the left hand to make the interphone more accessible. It is impossible for a gunner in full flying clothing to bring either hand up to the level of his face as there is not sufficient room between his chest and the turret structure. This means that it is possible to clear a gun stoppage or change a reflector sight bulb only by getting out of the turret. When the turret is rotated ahead of the beam position the full force of the slipstream is felt through the gun slots and this makes it essential for gunners to wear goggles firmly strapped in position. It is not considered advisable to fit panels in the gun slots unless these are made of perspex, as they would restrict the search view.

B-25Ds in formation. Powered by two 1,700 horse power Wright Cyclone 14 radials, this bomber had a maximum speed of 284 mph; carrying 2,000 pounds of bombs, it had an effective operational radius of about 700 miles.

Under-Turret

General. The Bendix under-turret is fully electric with two .5-in Browning guns with an ammunition supply of 330 rounds per gun. For take-off and landing it is fully retracted and almost flush with the fuselage. The turret is extended down a worm gear and takes $1\frac{1}{4}$ minutes to reach the fully 'down' position when 360 degree rotation and 90 degree depression become possible.

Sighting. Sighting is by means of a periscope with a prism at the bottom which rotates with the turret. By this means the gunner remains stationary with his eye to the sorbo rubber eyepiece, while the lower part of the turret with the guns and ammunition revolves. The field of view is a cone of 40 degrees and vision is clear at the beginning of the flight. The sighting panel is liable, however, to become spotted with oil which comes from various parts of the turret, the engines and an overflow vent on the port side of the fuselage. A Ki-gas pump has been fitted which enables the gunner to keep the sight clear. The rubber positioning pad for the eye is fairly comfortable but the eye freedom is small and the target is frequently lost during evasive action. When the guns are fired the vibration of the turret and sight is such that only very short bursts are possible. The sight is tiring to use and it is possible to maintain search for only very short periods.

Handling. The turret controls are very sensitive and there is no adequate slow speed for movement of the guns through a small angle. The result is that turret manipulation is jerky and although this could be improved with practice, it is very doubtful if sufficient control for accurate shooting could ever be obtained. Cine camera results show that fairly good shooting can be obtained at a 'no-deflection' target, but that as soon as the fighter breaks away, aiming becomes wild and inaccurate.

Firing tests. Firing was carried out on the stop butts and fair results were obtained with a burst of 5 rounds per gun. When ten rounds were fired, however, the jump became severe and the grouping bad, with a spread of 5 feet diameter at 40 yards. Some air firing was carried out which confirmed this impression although the guns themselves functioned well and there were no stoppages.

Gunner's Comfort. When the turret is extended the gunner is in a kneeling position, leaning forward over the turret at an angle of about 45 degrees with his weight supported by a chest pad. It was found that the turret manipulation — which presents a view of the ground revolving in a series of jerks — together with the pressure on the lungs due to the chest pad, in a short time made the gunner feel sick and while this might not occur to all individuals, it is a serious drawback on operations when a high state of efficiency is necessary.

Evasive Action. The Mitchell is capable of extremely violent evasive action when operating singly and the 'g' imposed is such that it is impossible for the under-gunner to use the turret owing to his semi-prone position and the small eye-freedom of the sight.

Front Gun

The .3-in Browning in the nose has three alternative positions with gimbal mountings, one pointing ahead, one on the port side and one pointing downwards. Each has a cone of fire of about 45 degrees but the gun position is of value only for scare purposes. A ring and bead sight is fitted and six magazines of 100 rounds each are carried.

Armour

The pilots' seats are protected by shaped armour $9\frac{1}{2}$mm thick, stretching from the head to the waist. A bulkhead of $9\frac{1}{2}$mm armour with a hinged door is provided across the whole fuselage immediately behind the rear compartment and a small piece of similar armour is fitted beneath the bomb-aimer's seat. The petrol tanks are self-sealing but the oil tanks have no protection.

Flying Characteristics

The Mitchell II is very similar in its flying characteristics to the Boston III. All controls are extremely positive at speeds up to 300 mph indicated. The aircraft can be flown comfortably on one engine and can be trimmed to fly 'hands off' as the trim tabs are very efficient.

Range, Speed and Consumption

The total fuel carried is 524 Imperial gallons in four wing tanks and the operational range at 15,000 feet at economical cruising speed is approximately 1,000 miles.

Fighting Tactics

All forms of evasive manoeuvre can be carried out with ease. A very tight turn is possible, and the corkscrew is also effective owing to the extreme manoeuvrability of the aircraft and the fact that negative 'g' can be imposed without cutting the engines. Skidding can be a useful manoeuvre as this can be done very violently at all speeds owing to the sensitiveness of the rudders. Fighting control must be carried out from the upper turret, as the astro-dome in the navigator's compartment has not sufficient field of view. The running commentary is also essential for the under-gunner as he is unable to search for any length of time through his periscopic sight.

Slipstream

The slipstream is exceptionally strong and makes it extremely difficult for a fighter to keepp his sights 'on' when within 300 yards astern.

Formation and Low Flying

Owing to the positiveness of the controls and the pilot's good field of view, formation and low flying are easy.

'The only real flaw in what Douhet said was that it did not allow for what would happen if the enemy took some elementary measures to defend potential targets...' The Hamburg Flak defences in action. *IWM*

3. The Tactics of Destruction

War is not an affair of chance.

FREDERICK THE GREAT

Strategic or Tactical?

Before we consider the nature of bomber tactics during the Second World War, it might be as well to settle on definitions for a couple of terms which too often have been used loosely: strategic bombing and tactical bombing.

The generally accepted definition of strategic bombing is: those bombing operations designed to effect the progressive destruction and disintegration of the enemy's capacity to make war. The definition of tactical bombing is: those bombing operations carried out in co-ordination with surface forces which directly assist the land or naval battle. The US Strategic Bombing Survey illustrated the differences in more graphic terms:

'Strategic bombing bears the same relationship to tactical bombing as does the cow to the pail of milk. To deny immediate aid and comfort to the enemy, tactical considerations dictate upsetting the bucket. To ensure eventual starvation, the strategic move is to kill the cow.'

If one accepts the above definitions, it is clear that the only factor which differentiates a strategic bombing attack from a tactical bombing attack is *the nature of the target*. It is true that the vast majority of strategic bombing attacks were carried out by heavy bombers flying over long ranges, just as the vast majority of tactical bombing attacks were flown by light or medium bombers flying over short ranges. But neither the size of the bombers involved, nor the distance flown, dictated whether an attack was strategic or tactical. Thus, when the US Navy launched striking forces of single-engined carrier-borne aircraft against Japanese aircraft factories from ranges of about 100 miles, during the early part of 1945, it was

undertaking *strategic* bombing operations. Similarly, when the Royal Air Force dispatched Lancaster bombers in November 1944 to strike at the German battleship *Tirpitz* in Tromso Fjord, 1,100 miles away from its bases in the north of Scotland (twice as far as Berlin was from the bases in Lincolnshire), it was undertaking *tactical* bombing operations. Moreover, while bombing attacks can be strategic or tactical in nature, it is misleading and inaccurate to fit types of bomber rigidly into such categories.

Defences: The Governing Factor in Bomber Tactics

Having defined strategic and tactical bombing attacks, let us now examine the effect the enemy defences had on the tactics used for either type of attack. The tactics employed by bombers during a particular operation usually depended on several quite unrelated factors: the nature of the object to be destroyed, the nature and strength of the defences, the type of bombs to be used, the distance between the base and the target, and the performance and armament of the bombers involved. Of these factors, however, it was almost invariably the defences that played the most important part in deciding the tactics to be employed.

Consider the bomber crews' ideal: the completely undefended target. To hit this, there was little need for tactical subtlety. The bombers could attack by day from low altitude, flying slowly so that the bomb aimers could plant their loads with great accuracy. It was this type of attack that Giulio Douhet had in mind in 1921, when he wrote in his famous book *The Command of the Air*:

'As an illustration of the magnitude of aerial power, let us assume that 100 kilogrammes of active material is capable of destroying the area of a circle 25 metres in radius. This supposition is consistent with present practice. Then, in order to extend the destructive action of this active material over a surface 500 metres in diameter, 100 times 100 kilogrammes, or 10 tons, will be required. Now, 10 tons of active material requires 10 tons of metal casing or shell. Today there are aeroplanes which can easily carry 2 tons of bombs in addition to their crews; ten such planes could carry all the bombs necessary to destroy everything within this circle of 500 metres diameter. To obtain this result it is necessary only to train the crews of ten aeroplanes to drop their bombs as uniformly as possible over that area.'

It was a persuasive line of argument and mathematically it was perfect. The only real flaw in what Douhet said was that it did not allow for what would happen if the enemy took some elementary measures to defend potential targets. A few light anti-aircraft guns round a target could inflict serious losses on bombers making individual low speed attacks from altitudes below 6,000 feet; a few heavy anti-aircraft guns could extend this zone of danger to 15,000 feet. As a 'rule of thumb', the risk of being hit by ground fire decreased by about a half for each 5,000 feet in altitude of the bombers, above 10,000 feet; for this reason, as anti-aircraft guns became more efficient, bombers were forced to attack from greater altitudes. Even if cloud or haze did not get in the way (as they frequently did), high altitude attacks were considerably less accurate than those from low altitude. Throw in a few fighters, and the bombers would have to carry machine guns and gunners for their defence at the expense of bomb load; to concentrate their defensive fire-power the raiders would have to fly in formation, which devoured fuel during the form-up and further reduced the weight of bombs that could be carried over a given distance.

If the combination of fighter and gun defences was powerful enough the raiders might be forced, as in the case of the Royal Air Force and the Luftwaffe early in the war, to abandon altogether large-scale daylight attacks beyond the range of escorting fighters. By night air defences tended to be far less effective, but until very late in the war night attacks were in general of a considerably lower order of accuracy than those by day; there was even a chance that a fair proportion of the bombers would fail to find their target at all. Thus the strengthening defences ruled out any possibility of crews dropping '...their bombs as uniformly as possible ...' over the area of the target, as Douhet had suggested; instead, the problem became the more basic one of enabling bomber crews to hit the target at all. Moreover, from the beginning of 1941, when radar-directed guns and night fighters began to join the defences in large numbers, the night attacks gradually ceased being a walk-over.

So it was that bombers came to attack from high altitude, or under cover of darkness, to render the defences less effective. A further variation was to approach the target at low altitude, to achieve surprise and possibly to avoid the defences altogether; we shall now examine some of the possibilities in this area of tactics.

Low Cunning

As every schoolbody now knows, the best way to avoid radar detection is to fly low. Against aircraft flying below about 5,000 feet, the range of ground radar stations is greatly reduced; if they are below 1,000 feet, continuous tracking is impossible unless stations are situated close together over a wide area. The defenders' problems can be further increased by the clever use of terrain: after the curvature of the earth, the best thing to screen an aircraft from radar detection is a hill or a mountain.

Since it is a classic in the annals of bomber routeing, we shall now examine the route used by the Royal Air Force Lancaster bombers which attacked the German battleship *Tirpitz* on November 12th 1944. Surprise was essential

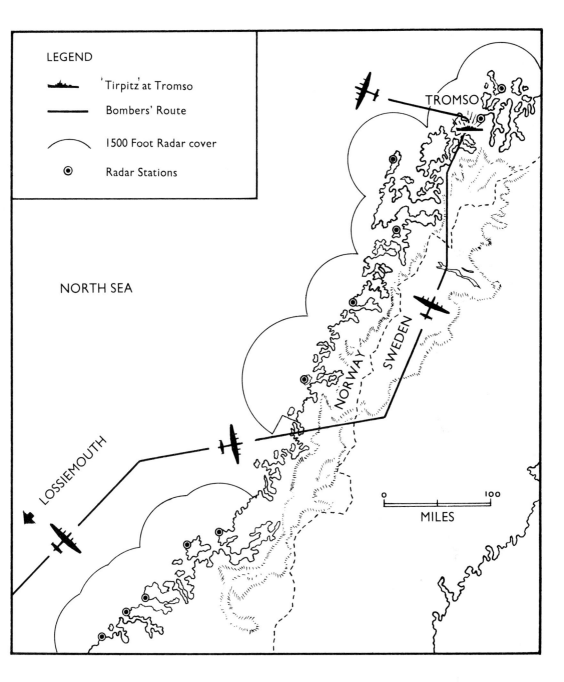

The low-altitude route to the *Tirpitz*, flown by Royal Air Force Lancaster bombers during the attack on November 12th 1944.

if this attack was to succeed. To hit the ship the bombers had to attack by day from altitudes around 12,000 feet. There were fighters based close to the anchorage used by *Tirpitz* and, so far as the RAF planners knew, there might also be smoke generators round the ship to screen her and make precision bombing impossible (in fact, these had not been moved into position).

As part of the general RAF effort to follow the continual changes in the German radar chain, electronic reconnaissance aircraft had

plotted the locations and arcs of cover of the stations in Norway. As was to be expected, against aircraft flying at 5,000 feet and above there was continual cover along the entire coast. If the bombers stayed below 1,500 feet, however, there was a small chink in the radar curtain in the centre of Norway. Behind the coast lay a mountain barrier, and beyond that lay neutral territory.

On examining these features, the RAF planners perceived a gap in the battleship's warning screen that could be exploited. The bombers were ordered to stay below 1,500 feet and make for the gap in the radar cover. They then continued almost due eastwards over the mountains and crossed into the country to the east of Norway. Keeping the screening mountain barrier between themselves and the prying German radar stations, the bombers

Wing Commander J.B. Tait (centre, not wearing flying kit) pictured with his crew after leading the successful attack which destroyed the *Tirpitz*.

turned on to a north-easterly heading which took them towards *Tirpitz* 'from the back'. Delaying their climb until the last moment, the bombers arrived over the battleship unhindered by enemy fighters and carried out an accurate attack from 12,000 feet. They scored three direct hits with 12,000 pound bombs which started uncontrollable fires deep inside the ship; when these reached one of the magazines there was a tremendous explosion which tore a long gash in the battleship's side. *Tirpitz* capsized.

Afterwards, Sir Ralph Cochrane, the commander of No 5 Bomber Group at the time of the *Tirpitz* operation, stated that it was the riskiest attack he had ever mounted. Had the

German defences operated properly, his bombers would have been shot out of the sky. The risks proved fully justified, however, and for the loss of only one aircraft to anti-aircraft fire *Tirpitz* was destroyed.

From the point of view of bomber routeing, the *Tirpitz* attack is noteworthy in five important respects. Firstly, the use of electronic reconnaissance: prior to the attack the German radar cover had been systematically mapped to seek out any possible gaps. Secondly, the use of a low altitude penetration to reduce the effective range of the German radars. Thirdly, the use of a route which exploited the gap which had been found in the defences. Fourthly, the use of a mountain range to screen the bombers from the German radars once they were over land. And fifthly, the rather clever use of the country to the east of Norway. Now, in the 1970s, the low altitude penetration is the most-used method of avoiding enemy defences; yet there has been little improvement in technique since the attack on *Tirpitz* in 1944.

All Together Now

If there were no defences to contend with, there would be little point in having bombers fly in formation. Flying in formation consumed fuel during the form-up, and more still due to the need for aircraft to accelerate and decelerate continually to hold position in formation; as a result, when they flew in formation, the bombers carried a reduced bomb load to all but the closest of targets. Moreover heavily laden aircraft were difficult to fly in formation, especially at high altitude, and this greatly increased pilot fatigue. Since attacks when there were no defences to fear were virtually unknown during the Second World War, however, some form of bunching was usual except during the early night attacks.

During daylight attacks, flying in close formation conferred two great advantages: firstly, it enabled the bombers to concentrate their fire against attacking fighters; and secondly it diluted the enemy gun defences, by presenting a multitude of simultaneous targets

rather than a succession of single ones that could be picked off more easily. And, if the bombers were lucky enough to have their own escorting fighters, these could protect a formation far more easily than individual aircraft.

Bombers could join formation relatively easily at low altitude, then climb to attack height *en route* to their target; this method was used by the Germans during the Battle of Britain. The bombers took off in close succession, either in Vics of three from grass airfields or else singly from concrete runways and formed into Vics soon after getting airborne. The Vics flew straight and level away from the airfield for a set time, then the leading Vic doubled back to the airfield collecting the succeeding Vics on the way. By the time they passed the airfield on the way back the bombers were in formation; they then turned on to their heading for the target and began their climb.

A low-altitude form-up had the advantage of simplicity. It also had the great disadvantage, however, that if there was cloud the formation had to climb through it. Climbing a formation of heavily laden bombers through cloud was not only difficult but dangerous, and it was not something to be undertaken lightly. A more practicable method, employed by the US Army Air Force when there was cloud, was for the bombers to take off and climb through cloud individually, then form up above cloud over a radio beacon. This method worked well enough, though it did take time: to form up at 8,000 feet overhead a radio beacon a B-17 Group with thirty-six aircraft required about an hour — which meant a reduction in the bombers' effective radius of action of about a hundred miles, or a reduction in the bomb load carried of some 1,700 pounds.

So far as the actual formations went, the requirements were roughly the same as they had been for military units throughout the history of warfare: to bring the maximum fire (or spear) power to bear on the enemy and give the chaps a feeling of togetherness, without having people get in each others' way. For bomber formations, the most-used element was the three-aircraft Vic. Five-aircraft Vics were

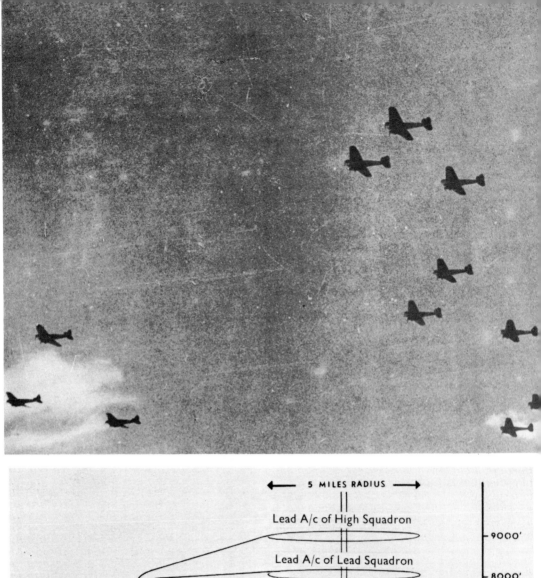

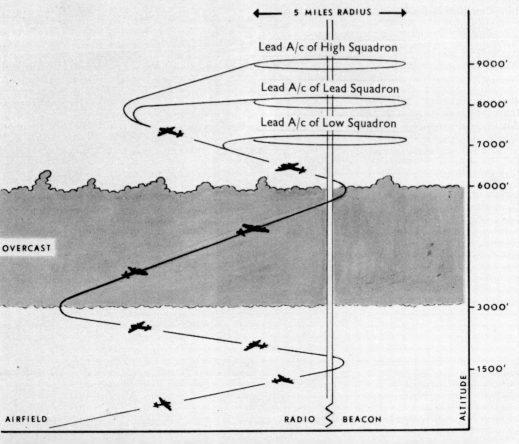

5 MILES RADIUS

Lead A/c of High Squadron — 9000'

Lead A/c of Lead Squadron — 8000'

Lead A/c of Low Squadron — 7000'

6000'

OVERCAST

3000'

1500'

AIRFIELD

RADIO BEACON

ALTITUDE

Heinkel 111s in a *Gruppenkeil*, a type of formation frequently used by German bombers. The leading aircraft took off and flew straight ahead for a set time, then doubled back to the airfield collecting the succeeding aircraft on the way; by the time the leading bomber regained the airfield, the succeeding aircraft were formed up behind. The formation then set course for the target and began its climb to attack altitude. *Dierich*

sometimes used, but with the larger aircraft there tended to be a 'concertina' effect which made this type of formation tiring to fly.

The Americans did far more work than anyone else to develop efficient types of formation for bombers. We shall, therefore, examine the steps taken by the US 8th Air Force to evolve types of formation to meet specific requirements. The importance of bombers maintaining formation can hardly be over-emphasised. During a survey carried out by the USAAF in 1943, it was shown that just over half of all the heavy bombers lost during

Opposite, below: Since it was dangerous for a formation of heavily-laden bombers to try to ascend through cloud, the US 8th Air Force evolved this system for forming up above cloud. For thirty-six bombers to form up in this way, however, it took over an hour.

Below & right: This type of formation was used by the US 8th Air Force during its initial attacks in August 1942. The aircraft flew in six-aircraft squadrons, with the squadrons widely separated.

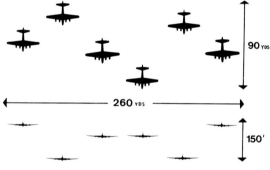

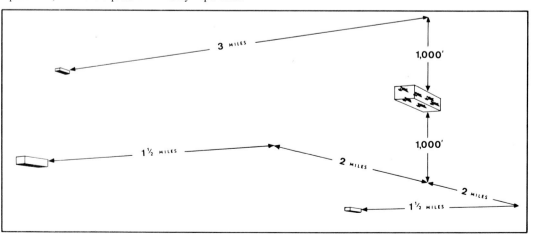

attacks on targets in Europe were shot down after they had left the formation for one reason or another. Until the final year of the war, when there were sufficient escorts to provide cover, American bombers straggling over German-held territory rarely survived.

When the 8th Air Force attacks began, in August 1942, the bombers flew in six-aircraft squadron formations. Within the squadrons the pilots flew about 100 feet (one wing-span) away from the nearest point of the aircraft in front. This gave 70 feet clear between the tail of the leading aircraft and the wing tip of the one following, a distance which gave a good compromise between concentration of defensive fire-power and ease of flying; moreover, this distance was great enough to ensure that a shell bursting between two bombers had little chance of causing fatal damage to both of them. The squadrons flew in a widely separated pattern, however. Thus, although the form-up was easy and the formation handled well, there was no mutual support between squadrons if one of them came under fighter attack. Moreover, the fire-power from a squadron of six heavy bombers proved insufficient to discourage German fighter pilots from pressing home attacks.

The need to provide a greater concentration of defensive fire-power led to a rapid revision in formation tactics and in September 1942 the American bombers began attacking in 18-aircraft Groups. The Group was split into two squadron boxes each of nine aircraft; the second squadron flew 500 feet above the leading one, slightly behind and echeloned away from the sun. This type of formation was more compact than the original one, but it was far less flexible. During turns the outside aircraft could lose sight of the leader; also, because the aircraft in each squadron flew at the same altitude, there were frequent occasions when they blocked each others' fields of fire.

To improve matters, a revised Group formation was introduced in December 1942. The 18-aircraft Group remained, but now comprised three squadrons each of six aircraft. The bombers flew stacked towards the sun, with the leading squadron in the centre and the high and low squadrons trailing slightly behind. This change unmasked many guns and improved the Group's effective fire-power. By this time the 8th Air Force was expanding rapidly and could now send up to four such Groups into action. Succeeding Groups followed each other at 1½ mile intervals in a so-called 'Javelin', flying slightly above the one in front and echeloned towards the sun. The intention with the 'Javelin' was to make it difficult for German fighters to take the best line of approach when making head-on attacks on aircraft in the rear Groups. The disadvantage of the 'Javelin' was that with succeeding Groups stacked in trail at increasing altitudes, the high aircraft had difficulty in keeping up. There tended to be stringing-out and the resultant stragglers became an easy prey for the German fighters.

In February 1943, the 'Javelin' of Groups gave way to the 'Wedge'. The 18-aircraft Group formation remained as before but the leading Group was placed in the centre of the formation with following Groups stacked above in echelon and below in echelon in the opposite direction. By placing the leading Group at mid-altitude it reduced the speed differential between the leader and the highest Group, reducing but not eliminating the tendency for the latter's aircraft to straggle.

By March 1943 the increasing intensity of the attacks by German fighters led to a further change in the bomber formations. Now the need was for the greatest possible defensive fire-power. Still the 18-aircraft Group formation remained unchanged, but now three such Group formations were placed close together: following the lead Group was one immediately behind, to one side and above, with another immediately behind to the other side and below. The resultant 54-aircraft Combat Wing formation was about one and a third miles wide, half a mile deep and a third of a mile from front to rear. It gave greatly increased fire-power and mutual support between aircraft, squadrons and Groups; at the same time, however, it was unwieldy and particularly difficult to hold in the turn, when the aircraft in

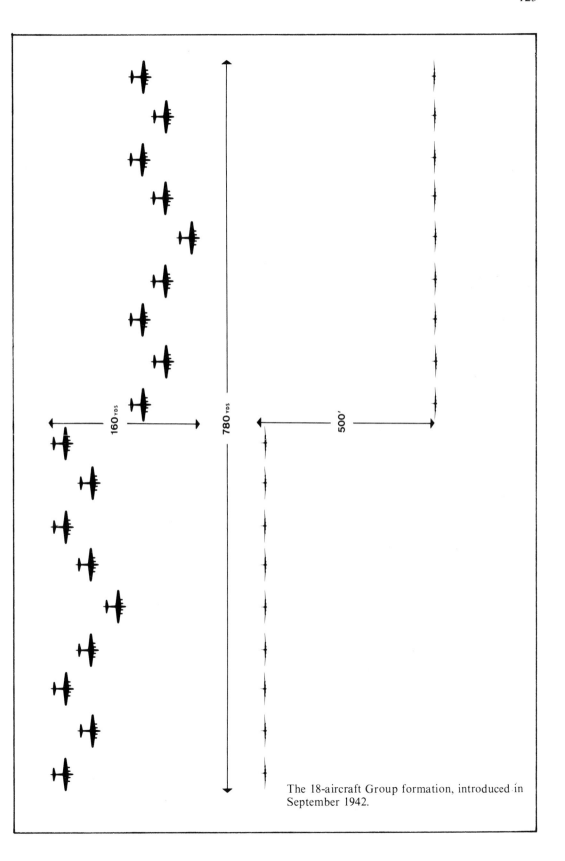

The 18-aircraft Group formation, introduced in September 1942.

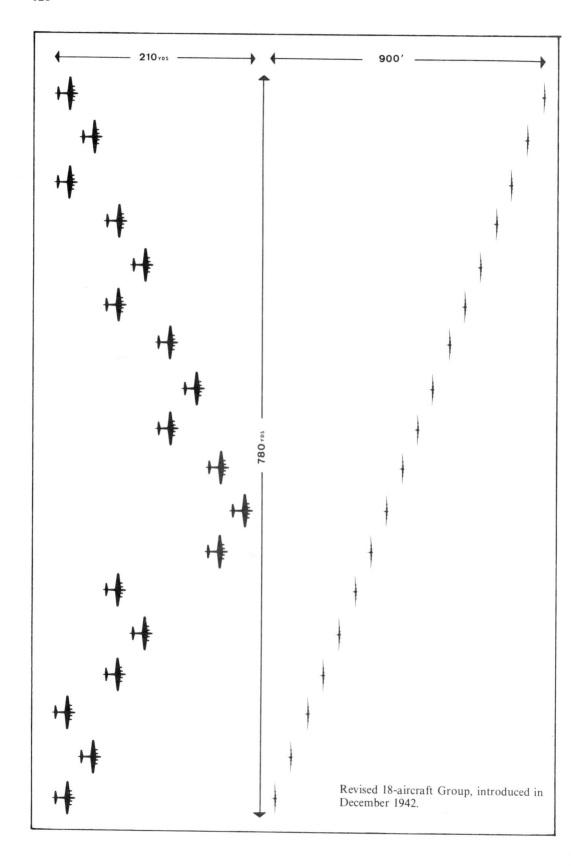

210 YDS

900'

780 YDS

Revised 18-aircraft Group, introduced in December 1942.

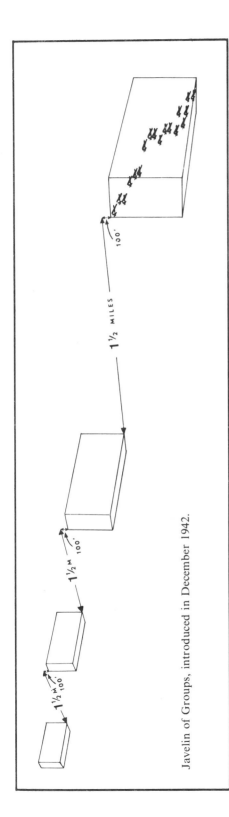

Javelin of Groups, introduced in December 1942.

the high Group had difficulty in keeping the leaders in view. Combat Wing formations followed each other at 6-mile intervals.

In April 1943 moves were made to bring the 54 aircraft in the Combat Wing formation still closer together. The high and low squadrons and Groups were tucked in closer behind the leaders. At the same time the three-aircraft Vics were stacked in one direction while both the elements and the squadrons were stacked in the opposite direction. The resultant 'tucked-in' Wing formation afforded greater lateral compression and increased still further the concentration of defensive fire-power and the degree of mutual support between aircraft and units. This type of formation was to serve the 8th Air Force throughout the greater part of 1943, which saw the hardest-fought deep-penetration attacks into Germany.

During the closing months of 1943 there were two fundamental changes in the nature of the American bomber attacks on Germany: firstly, there was the increasing availability of escort fighters with the range to provide cover to and from targets; secondly, there was the introduction of radar aids to bombing. With the escort fighters providing the bombers' first line of protection, concentrated defensive fire-power was no longer all-important; moreover, a formation of smaller overall dimensions was easier both for the bombers to hold and the fighters to escort. At the same time the initial shortage of radar equipment meant that only a few of the bombers carried it; to make the most of what there was, a change was made to a 12-aircraft squadron formation with the radar-fitted machine in the lead. The new formation was introduced in January 1944; three such squadron formations made up a 36-aircraft Group, and Groups followed each other at four-mile intervals.

The 36-aircraft Group remained in use from the beginning of 1944 until the end of the war, though early in 1945 there was a revision in the shape of the formation. By this time the German fighter force was no longer a serious danger; but the Germans had intensified the use of Flak and this now posed the main threat to the bombers. The requirement was now for a

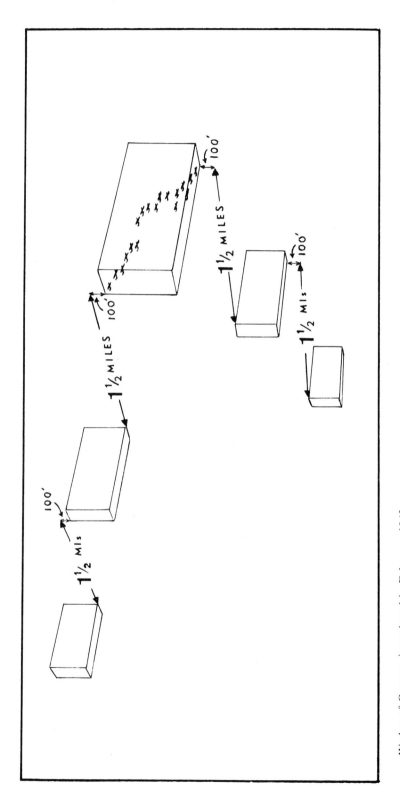

Wedge of Groups, introduced in February 1943.

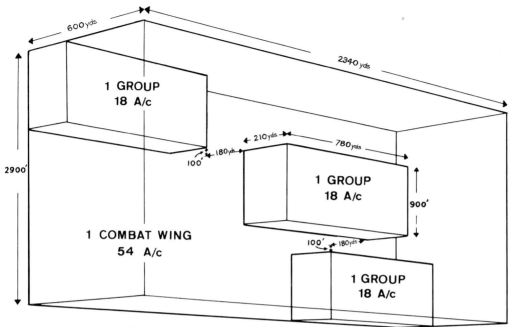

600 yds

2340 yds

1 GROUP
18 A/c

210 yds

780 yds

180 yds

100'

2900'

900'

1 GROUP
18 A/c

1 COMBAT WING
54 A/c

100' 180 yds

1 GROUP
18 A/c

The 54-aircraft Combat Wing Formation,
introduced in March 1943.

formation which could easily be escorted but which provided the most difficult target for Flak. Also at this time, there was no longer any shortage of radar-equipped bombers. In February 1945 the 8th Air Force revised its Group formation, using four squadrons each of nine aircraft instead of the earlier three squadrons each with twelve. The new Group formation had a greater vertical extent, which made it more difficult for the Flak gunners to shift their fire from one squadron to another; it was also easier to hold, with the result that there were fewer stragglers. This type of Group formation remained in use in the majority of 8th Air Force units until the end of the war.

The above description is not intended to cover every single type of formation tried by the 8th Air Force. It does, however, show some of the steps taken to evolve formations to keep pace with the continually changing military situation.

It must be stressed that everything said about formation flying applies only to daylight bomber attacks. Not only was night formation flying extremely difficult, but only rarely could its use confer any tactical advantage. With visibility on a dark night limited to about 200 yards if the enemy fighter was above the horizon, and far less if it was below the horizon, there was unlikely to be any opportunity for one bomber to provide defensive support for its neighbour; and considerably lower concentrations of bombers were sufficient to provide far more targets than the defences could engage simultaneously.

The so-called 'bomber streams' employed by the RAF are sometimes talked about as though they were formations, but such a description is grossly misleading. The pilots did not rely on visual contact to hold position on their neighbours; instead, each navigator was given a route and timing points and told to do his best to adhere to these. Since aerial navigation was still an inexact science and crews could rarely refer to ground features, the bombers in the stream were spread over a wide area. For example, taking a typical RAF night attack in the summer of 1943, the majority of the 650 bombers involved were spread over a rectangular-shaped volume of sky 150 miles long, six miles wide and two miles deep; on the fringes, there would be aircraft more than 30

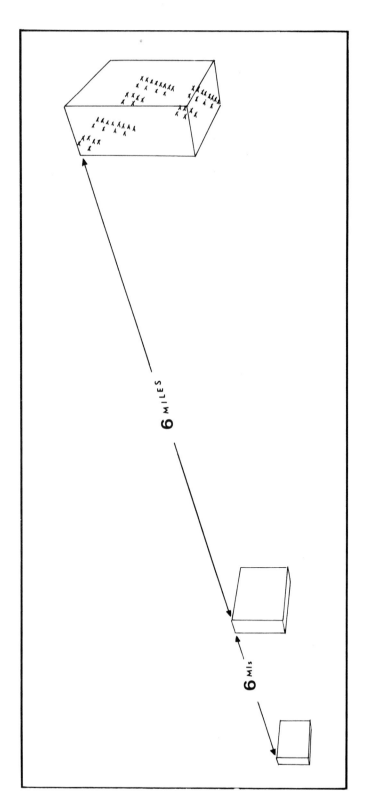

Combat Wing Formations following each other at 6-mile intervals.

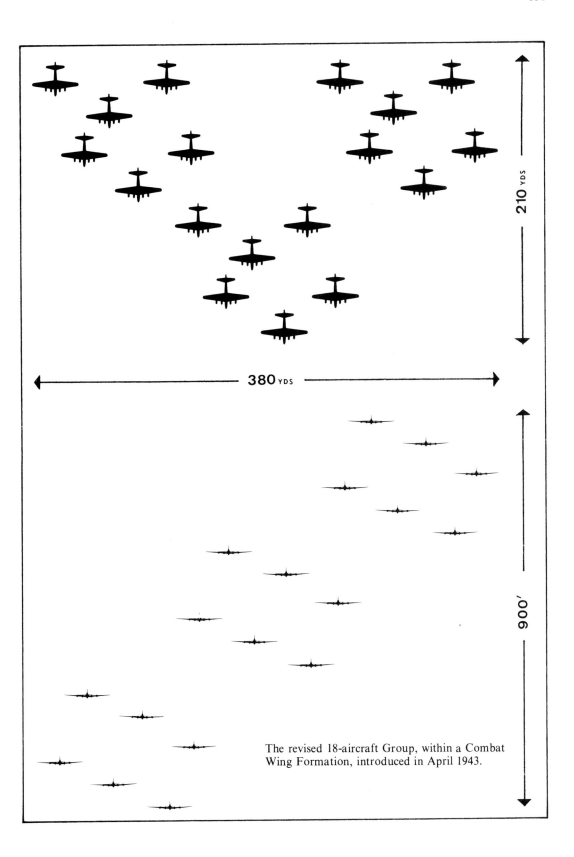

The revised 18-aircraft Group, within a Combat Wing Formation, introduced in April 1943.

380 YDS · 210 YDS · 900′

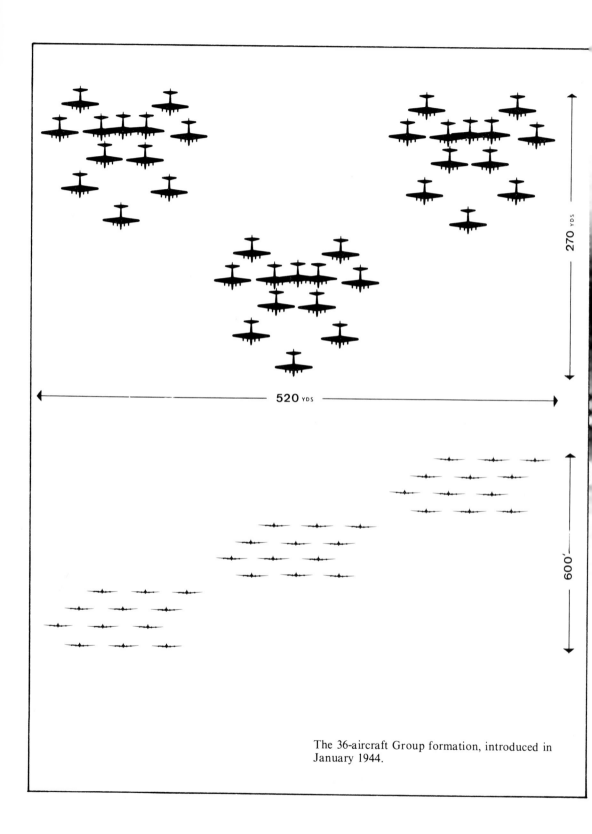

The 36-aircraft Group formation, introduced in January 1944.

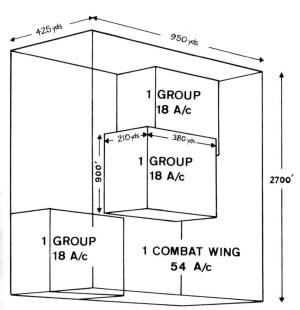

The 'tucked-in' 54-aircraft Combat Wing Formation, introduced in April 1943.

miles off the planned route. What sort of aircraft density did this produce at the centre of the stream? If the base of this page can be taken to represent a distance of one mile, a single heavy bomber to this scale would be about the size of a letter 'T'; at the centre of the stream there would be an average of between one and two such 'T-sized' aircraft, within an area the size of this page. By the end of the war bomber streams were flying at densities four times as great as this; but it can be seen that this was a 'same way same day' type of flying, rather than a formation in the normal sense of the word. The use of the bomber stream conferred little or no fuel or bomb load penalty, compared with individually-routed aircraft, but it gave a degree of concentration high enough to complicate greatly the task of the radar-directed Flak and fighter defences.

Tactics for Survival

When they were intercepted by enemy fighters, bombers relied on their speed, altitude, manoeuvrability of fire-power, or a combination of these, for survival.

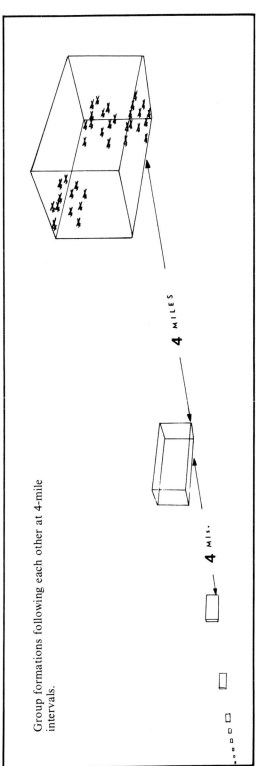

Group formations following each other at 4-mile intervals.

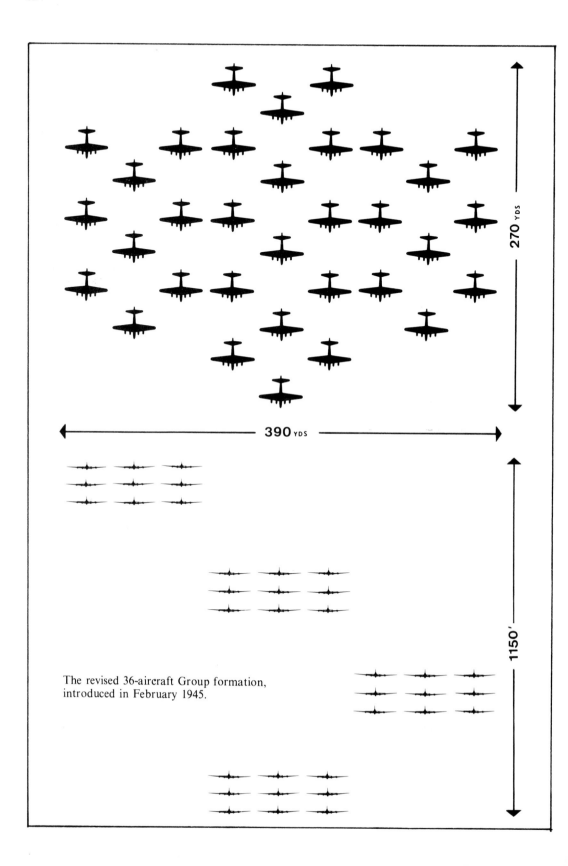

The revised 36-aircraft Group formation,
introduced in February 1945.

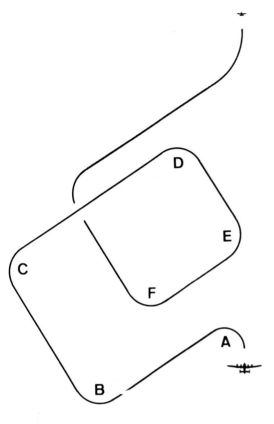

The 'Corkscrew' evasive manoeuvre which enabled a bomber to continue on its route while at the same time presenting an attacking fighter with the most difficult target possible. The manoeuvre depicted was the one specific to the Lancaster bomber in 1945, and would follow the sighting of a fighter attacking from port.

A The pilot opened his throttles, banking at 45 degrees and making a diving turn to port; the bomber descended through about 1,000 feet in six seconds. During the dive, the bomber's speed increased from about 230 mph to nearly 300 mph.

B After descending 1,000 feet the pilot pulled the aircraft into a climb, still turning to port.

C Half way up the climb the turn was reversed; in the climb the speed fell away rapidly, which often caused an attacking fighter to overshoot.

D By the time it reached its original altitude, the bomber's speed was down to about 185 mph. Still in the starboard turn, the nose was pushed down and the aircraft commenced a further dive.

E In the dive the bomber picked up speed again. After descending through about 500 feet, the direction of the turn was reversed.

F If the fighter was still present, the manoeuvre was repeated.

The American daylight bombers were heavily armed and we have already seen the trouble the 8th Air Force went to in evolving formations which would provide concentrated fire-power. When such bombers came under attack they continued flying straight and level, holding their tight formation and relying on their guns to ward off the fighters.

Co-ordinated manoeuvring in order to avoid fighter attack was normally limited to small independently-operating formations of up to four aircraft, by bombers carrying a moderately heavy defensive armament. Such tactics were often used by day bombers operating in small numbers; the most effective tactics have been outlined in Chapter 2 (see page 100).

For aircraft operating singly, whatever their type, the so-called 'Corkscrew' manoeuvre was found to be the most effective when a fighter intercepted. This manoeuvre gave the best possible compromise between getting the bomber to and from its target, and giving the fighter the most difficult shot. If executed early enough and with sufficient vigour, the corkscrew alone was sufficient to render night bombers almost immune from fighter attack; indeed, the more experienced German night fighter pilots would often break away from 'Corkscrewing' bombers and try to surprise another aircraft in the bomber stream, rather than engage in a long and usually fruitless chase on such a difficult target.

Delivering the 'Nasties'

When the bombers reached their target, the type of attack depended largely on the nature of the object to be hit. If it was a hardened target, heavily protected either by steel armour or concrete, the armour piercing bombs had to be released from high altitude or they would not have reached a great enough speed during their fall to get them through the hardening. Similarly, if the target was a very small one, such as a tank or a small ship, high level bombing was not accurate enough and a low altitude attack was necessary to give a reasonable chance of scoring a hit.

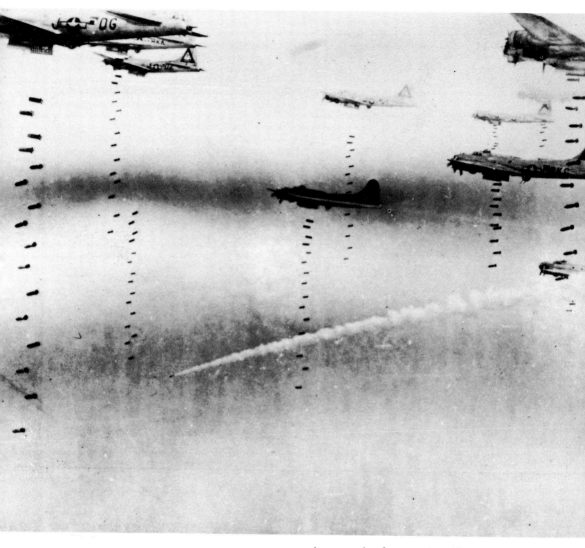

Terms such as 'glide bombing', 'skip bombing' and 'dive bombing' are often used loosely. In this account, the main attack methods are defined as follows:

Horizontal Bombing: the bombs were released while the aircraft was flying straight and level at low, medium or high altitude. Low altitude horizontal bombing using delayed action bombs was sometimes referred to as 'skip bombing'.

Shallow Glide Bombing: the bombs were released while the aircraft was descending at an angle not greater than 20 degrees.

An example of pattern bombing: B-17s of the 384th Bomb Group seen releasing their bombs simultaneously, as a smoke marker falls from the lead aircraft. *USAF*

Steep Glide Bombing: the bombs were released while the aircraft was descending at an angle of between 20 and 60 degrees.

Dive Bombing: the bombs were released while the aircraft was in a dive at an angle of between 60 and 90 degrees.

Horizontal Bombing: Medium and high level horizontal attacks were the normal method for heavy bombers and the majority of medium

bombers; this type of attack was suitable only for those aircraft fitted with downward-looking sighting positions, or those equipped to make use of radar-bombing techniques. The accuracy of this type of attack deteriorated as bombing altitude was increased.

A variation of the high altitude horizontal attack was that termed 'pattern bombing' and used by the American heavy bomber formations. It was discovered early in the 8th Air Force's offensive that if bombers carried out individual attack runs when they reached the target, it tended to disrupt the carefully planned formations. Colonel, later General, Curtiss Le May was an early advocate of the pattern bombing techniques in which the pilots concentrated on holding their position on the leading aircraft and released their bombs on a signal from that aircraft's bombardier. This produced a concentrated pattern of bombs on the ground, aimed usually by the best bomb aimer in the unit. The method worked well, and

A leading advocate of pattern bombing in the US Army Air Force was Colonel, later General, Curtiss Le May (with cigar). This picture was taken early in 1945 when, holding the rank of Major General, Le May commanded the XXIth Bomber Command which was carrying out attacks on metropolitan Japan with B-29s. To the right of Le May is Brigadier General Thomas Powers, the commander of the B-29 units based on Guam. *USAF*

came to be used throughout the 8th Air Force. Its only real snag was that the German Flak gunners tended to show their admiration for those on board the leader's aircraft by concentrating their fire upon it.

For low altitude horizontal attacks the approach was made flying as low as possible, with the bombs released from altitudes of around 50 feet with the aircraft flying at full throttle. This method could be very accurate, giving 50 per cent errors during operations of the order of 50 yards for the initial impact point of the bomb. Such attacks could be very costly,

however, if the target was defended by light Flak and the element of surprise had been lost. Moreover, target identification could be difficult if the objective did not stand higher than the surrounding countryside.

When used with delayed action bombs, the low altitude horizontal attack was sometimes referred to as 'skip bombing'. For this type of attack a bomb firing delay of the order of ten seconds was essential, if the aircraft was not to risk damage from its own bombs. Skip attacks were suitable only against targets which were bulky enough to stop the bombs hurled against them and tall enough to catch any bombs which bounded high after the first impact; typical targets were hangars, large buildings, railway embankments and unarmoured ships. Unless they were stopped by the target, the bombs were liable to bounce considerable distances: during trials with 250 pound bombs released from 60 feet at 300 mph, there were cases when bombs bounced twice as high as the releasing

Skip bombing: a spectacular series of pictures, taken during an operation by B-25J Mitchells of the US 345th Bomb Group against Japanese escort vessels off Amoy on April 6th 1945. The aircraft attacked from altitudes around 100 feet, aiming the 5-second-delay fused 500 pound bombs at a point in the water just short of the target. During the action the Frigates Nos 1 and 34 (one of which is depicted) and the destroyer *Amatsukaze* were all sunk. *USAF*

aircraft and came to rest nearly three-quarters of a mile away from the first impact point.

One way of exploiting the accuracy of the low altitude horizontal attack, without the drama of the skip attack, was to use retarded bombs. A typical example of these was the 'Parafrag' weapon used by the US Army Air Force; released in clusters at low altitude, these 23 pound weapons were slowed by small parachutes and the releasing aircraft was safely clear by the time they struck the ground and went off.

Shallow Glide Bombing. In this type of attack the bomber released its bombs in a shallow glide, descending at an angle of up to 20 degrees. Bomb release altitude was usually below 2,000 feet and, if accuracy was all-important, it could be as low as 50 feet. Since this type of attack gave little chance of achieving surprise, it was potentially more risky for the bomber than the low altitude horizontal attack; moreover, the accuracy likely to be achieved was no greater. The shallow glide attack was really suitable only against ill-defended targets which were not tall enough to be seen clearly from aircraft flying horizontally at low altitude, or those against which large unretarded bombs were necessary which would otherwise bounce past the target.

A low altitude attack using retarded bombs: B-25 Mitchells of the US 5th Air Force seen releasing strings of 23-pound 'Parafrags', parachute-retarded fragmentation bombs, against parked Japanese aircraft during an attack on Dagua, New Guinea, in February 1944. *USAF*

Steep Glide Bombing. This method, in which the bombs were released in a glide descending at an angle of between 20 and 60 degrees, was the most practical form of attack for those bombers which lacked a downward-looking sighting position and which were not stressed or equipped to carry out dive attacks. There was no set altitude for bomb release. A typical attack using this method might commence from 11,000 feet, with bomb release at 8,500 feet so that the aircraft need not descend below

6,000 feet in the pull-out and could thus keep outside the range of accurate light Flak. A typical operational accuracy was a 50 per cent circular error of about 200 yards, if the release altitude was 8,500 feet. If the release altitude was 3,000 feet, giving a minimum altitude during the pull-out of 1,000 feet or lower, 50 per cent zones of 50 yards were possible but the attack was then as risky as the shallow glide.

Dive Bombing. For dive attacks, the bomber descended at angles between 60 and 90 degrees. For this type of attack to be employed by multi-engined aircraft, the machines had to be specially stressed for the pull-out and equipped with dive brakes to prevent the speed building up too much during the descent. As a result such aircraft descended slowly and pulled up sharply, compared with the more normal types

of bomber which were limited to steep glide attacks. As in the case of the steep glide attack, bombing accuracy was inversely proportional to release altitude; but the tighter pull-up meant that the dive bomber could release its bombs from a lower altitude with less risk from the ground defences.

Accurate estimation of side winds was very important for steep glide or diving attacks, if they were to achieve good results. An interesting ploy used by the Germans during such attacks on small targets was to have the first three aircraft in the attacking force bomb without allowing for the wind. Succeeding aircraft then used the bomb craters to judge the correct amount to aim off, so that their bombs would hit the target.

The Petlyakov Pe-2 high speed bomber was stressed and equipped to carry out dive-bombing attacks. Powered by two 1,100 VK-105 in-line engines, it had a maximum speed of 361 mph; carrying 2,000 pounds of bombs, it had an effective operational radius of about 150 miles. *IWM*

4. Summary

A battle is a swirl of 'ifs' and 'ands'.

SIR IAN HAMILTON

Despite the pre-war prophesies that 'The bomber will always get through', this type of aircraft proved extremely vulnerable when war came in 1939. At the end of the 1930s air defences had suddenly become much more effective. The significant new factor was radar, the long-range eye that provided warning to enable fighters to be positioned accurately to meet incoming bombers. Given this advantage, the fighter had a clear superiority over the bomber during the early part of the war.

At the beginning of the Second World War none of the bombers in service had the performance to avoid, nor the fire-power to defend themselves against, modern fighters. To survive, such bombers had to attack either by day with fighter escort, or else at night when initially the defences were inefficient and interception was unlikely. The shift to night attacks led to considerable advances in the development of electronic systems to enable bomber crews to find targets. Later, as the night defences became more and more effective, it became necessary for bombers to carry special equipment to prevent detection by, or cause confusion to, enemy defensive radar systems. By the end of the Second World War night

The German bomber ace Major Bernhard Jope shaking hands with Adolf Hitler, after being awarded the Oakleaves to the Ritterkreuz in March 1944. To the right of Jope stands Major Hans-George Baetcher, who was similarly decorated; Baetcher was to command *III./KG 76* during the jet bomber unit's short operational career. *Jope*

Arado 234s of the first true jet bomber unit to go
into action, the Third *Gruppe* of *Kampfgeschwader
76*, pictured during the winter of 1944. *KG 76
Archive*

attack had been developed to a fine art; but so too had night air defence.

On the question of long range bombers, the Americans took a different tack from everyone else. They had nailed their colours firmly to the mast of daylight precision bombing and pressed ahead with the development of the B-17 and B-24 bombers, which were intended to fight their way through the enemy defences to targets far beyond the reach of escorting fighters. This meant carrying batteries of heavy machine guns for self defence, with the result that these aircraft carried bomb loads considerably smaller than heavy bombers of other nations. At first the American heavy bombers were able to operate without suffering unacceptably heavy losses. But by the summer of 1943 the German fighter force had taken the measure of the threat and was able to inflict crippling losses on forces of bombers making deep penetrations into the Reich by day. The simple fact was that a fighter could bring to bear in one direction a fire-power overwhelmingly greater than that which a bomber could carry to defend itself against attacks from all directions. Fortunately for the US Army Air Force, however, their long range escort fighters became available right on cue and saved a humiliating climb-down by the daylight bombing protagonists.

A third avenue of approach was the development of the really high speed bomber, exemplified by the British de Havilland Mosquito and the German Arado 234. Such aircraft carried no defensive armament and relied on a combination of speed, altitude and evasive routing to avoid interception by enemy fighters.

At the close of the Second World War the zenith in design amongst bombers in service was represented by two types, the Boeing B-29 and the Arado 234.

In 1945 the B-29 was by a wide margin the largest and heaviest bomber in service. Alone amongst the heavy bombers at that time, it was fully effective both by day and by night: as standard equipment it carried the fire-power to enable it to give a good account of itself against enemy fighters, and the radar to enable it to bomb targets shrouded by cloud or darkness. Its combination of range and bomb-carrying capability were unequalled, and no heavy bomber came close to it in altitude performance. Compared with the best long range bomber in service at the beginning of the war, the same company's B-17A, the B-29 was able to carry six times the bomb load twice as far and attack from altitudes almost twice as high. For self-defence the B-29's two-gun barbettes each mounted twice the fire-power of a turret fitted to the Wellington, the best defended bomber in 1939; in the rear turret the B-29 carried two .5-in machine guns and a 20mm cannon, providing a fire-power twice as great as that of the dorsal position of the Loiré et Olivier 451. Moreover, due to the positioning of the B-29's guns which enabled at least two and sometimes as many as four gun positions to open fire against an approaching fighter, this superiority in fire-power over the 1939 bombers was compounded. Against the poorly armed and armoured Japanese fighters the B-29's guns performed impressively. Whether they would have been sufficient to ward off the best possible defence in 1945, namely a massed attack by Messerschmitt 262 jet fighters armed with heavy cannon and rockets, is open to doubt however. It is interesting to note that neither the cruising speed nor the attack speed of the B-29 was any great advance over those of the Loiré et Olivier 451, the fastest bomber in 1939.

The B-29 progressed from initial concept to large scale service in only four years; it was a powerful demonstration of what the Americans are capable of, if someone frightens them enough. The Russians bestowed upon the bomber the supreme compliment of copying it and placing it into large scale production. In 1948 the Tupolev 4, as it was renamed, entered service with Russian heavy bomber units and caused a profound shock in the west. The mounting of a defence to counter a possible massed attack by such bombers operating by night was to exercise British and American planners until the mid-1950s — not bad for an aircraft whose original design dated from 1940 and which had first entered service in 1943.